Christian Marriage

The New Challenge

David M. Thomas, Ph.D.

A Michael Glazier Book

LITURGICAL PRESS
Collegeville, Minnesota

www.litpress.org

A Michael Glazier Book published by Liturgical Press

The Scripture quotations are from the *New Revised Standard Version Bible*, Catholic edition, © 1989 by the Division of Christian Education of the National Council of Churches of Christ in the U.S.A. Used with permission. All rights reserved.

Cover design by Ann Blattner.

1   2   3   4   5   6   7   8   9

Library of Congress Cataloging-in-Publication Data

Thomas, David Michael, 1938–
    Christian marriage : the new challenge / David M. Thomas. — 2nd ed.
      p.   cm.
    "A Michael Glazier book."
    ISBN-13: 978-0-8146-5224-4
    ISBN-10: 0-8146-5224-7
    1. Marriage—Religious aspects—Catholic Church.   2. Catholic Church—Doctrines.   I. Title.

BX2250.T4555 2007
234'.165—dc22
                                                        2006019919

Contents

Introduction

Powerful winds of cultural change now blow with great force over the hallowed institutions of church and society. One of the places feeling the full force of these winds is marriage. They also fan a large cluster of issues that influence married life. Receiving the most public attention lately is whether government and religious bodies will sanction same-sex unions as marital. Some countries have given full rights and privileges to both heterosexual and same-sex unions. Marriage obviously has its benefits, both personal and legal. In the United States there is a movement to establish a constitutional amendment declaring marriage to be only between a woman and a man. The debate shows no signs of lessening.

Those looking for a resolution of this issue will not find it here. While I have deep respect for those on both sides of this issue, I chose to deal only with the terrain I know best, marriage between a man and a woman. My intent is to support traditional marriage with the best arguments and reflections I can. That's where I will focus my attention and energy. Besides I'm not the arguing type. I leave that to others who seem to enjoy controversy. From the start of this book, I focus on the challenges and rewards of heterosexual marriage. A positive side of the marriage debate is that it invites us to rethink basic questions. That's always a good move.

Other issues stirring the waters around marriage come from personal choices influenced by social and economic forces. Statistics indicate that fewer people of marital age are deciding to marry. One of the most interesting examples of this is the large number of elderly couples living together, but remaining unmarried "on the books." They fill retirement communities from southern Florida to the far west. If they married, they might lose needed financial benefits. Looking at the younger set, it is now a social norm for most that couples cohabit before entering married life in the eyes of family, friends, and state. Some will never marry although they will live together, beget children, and share most everything with each other, except marriage.

Quite a few years ago I was teaching a college course on Christian marriage and conducted an informal survey on the students' living arrangements. I was surprised to learn how many were at that time living together as preparation for eventual marriage. Wanting to know more, I asked them why. Most responded by telling me that they didn't want to make the same mistake as their parents. They saw their own actions as a better preparation for entering a lifelong union. The research seems to suggest that it's not that simple. Those who cohabit before marriage experience slightly higher divorce rates than those who do not. Like all the issues touching marriage, complexity reigns.

With all these new living arrangements, I wonder about the personal, social, and moral implications of these relationships. The world now offers us not only a hundred varieties of ice cream, but also almost as many lifestyles. Abundant arguments pro and con flow on all sides of these social situations. Eventually the debate includes a discussion of the very essence of marriage. Who would have even imagined a few years ago that marriage would become such a debated, even controversial, topic?

A little over twenty years ago I wrote a book called *Christian Marriage: A Journey Together*. At that time I was married and a young father. Now I'm a young grandfather and still married. Now I must write with an awareness of the changed world of the twenty-first century firmly in mind. Like everything human, marriage bears the imprint of the time in which it exists. The marriage of my wife and me and the marriages of those of our children are always evolving. And that's not a negative. They are alive, and a basic sign of life is change and adaptation to new circumstances. The river of life continues to flow.

For starters, marriage has moved from being a simple journey together (part of my original book title) to being an ever new, quite decisive challenge. As I write this updated account of Christian marriage, I must certainly be attentive to those many issues swirling around marriage. But I also want to pay careful attention to the personal lives of the married. I want my theological reflection on marriage to be grounded in real experience. The true experts in the spiritual and theological meaning of marriage are those who are married.

In Stephanie Coontz's recent book, *Marriage, A History*, she tells us that from the standpoint of society and from what's happening between married couples these days, there is nothing in the past that can equate with what's happening today. Nothing! She notes that more has changed in the last thirty years than in the previous three thousand years. That's a bold assertion, but I think she's basically right. Of course, she's using the tools of a social scientist to support her view. As a theologian, I would add that marriage also contains some important constants, a few essential characteristics that are part of all marriages. I would trace this back to God's creative intent for humankind. More about that later.

So what's it like when a couple announces to family and friends that they are getting married? What's going through their minds? Or those of their parents and friends? Is there delight, approval, concern—or a mixture of all three? Most would agree that getting married these days signals the taking of a big step involving no small amount of risk, especially if one is thinking of a lifelong union. And once married, the challenges might even escalate. No, I take that back. They *will* escalate. And given the variety of "social arrangements" or "quasi marriages" involving couples these days, maybe the act of getting married in traditional fashion may be thought of as almost countercultural.

Not too many years ago, society supported marriage as an institution, and religious bodies affirmed its value and importance without qualification. Thirty years ago more than 90 percent of adults in America married. That number has dropped. In the recent past, marital success was always thought of as no small achievement, but it was certainly not thought of as an impossible achievement. Today some would say it is. A few years ago virtually everyone in society saw marriage as an obvious good, a fully worthwhile way to live and beneficial to both those married and those around them. But times have changed. And like so many areas of life, while some of the changes appear to be positive, some seem negative.

Trained as a sociologist and a theologian, I'm always observing the interface between culture and religion. That's a big part of the framework I use when studying the rich phenomena of contemporary marriage. In my own list of primary cultural influences on marriage, I would include the presence of a growing desire for self-satisfaction that may or may not include the good of others. I see lifestyles geared primarily toward personal, individual survival. There are job-related requirements diminishing the time spent at home with family. The most recent studies of gainful employment show that workers in the United States work more hours each week than workers in any other country in the world. We recently overtook the Japanese. People seem to want more and are willing to work more to get it. People work hard to assure their own employment, too. There's little security these days in the world of work. Most of these "trends" seem to have a negative impact on marriage.

I see two specific societal developments that I would label as positive. First there is the almost universal view that marriage be based on mutual love. In Coontz's study of the history of marriage, we find compelling evidence that marriage throughout history existed much more in the worlds of politics, economics, and family needs than in the world of love. We would hope that love has been a part of marriage, no matter what the historical period. But it has not been a primary determining influence until the last century. And even then, its importance was not universal.

The coupling of marriage as a social institution with love between the wife and husband has been an important aspect in developing a theology and spirituality of marriage.

A second significant social trend is that of gender equality in marriage. Both giving and receiving form essential interpersonal dynamics in marriage. Clearly, this goes a long way to ensuring the full personal dignity of each spouse, a value strongly supported in contemporary theology.

You can see that my list of the positives and negatives touches on the basic value of respectful, loving interpersonal life. In a word, if marriage is in trouble, it's because as a society we are tending to push the "self-other" dynamic too much toward the side of the self. Marriage is essentially communal; our culture is becoming more and more individual. It doesn't have to be that way because the tilt toward the individual is directed by freely made decisions. But at the same time we continue to affirm the value of deep, interpersonal love. So some forces pull us apart; others draw us together. On this field, contemporary marriage unfolds. Also within marriage, spiritual possibilities of immense value to the persons involved and to God's loving Spirit unfold.

Chapter One

Why did God create marriage?

Children often ask the best questions. Like how can flies walk on the ceiling? Or how does the moon change its size? Or why are people different colors? They enter life with insatiable curiosity. Sadly, some of them lose it much too soon.

Theology, the academic field I work in, also moves under the power of good questions. Most of them include questions about God. Why did God create the universe? Or what was God like before creation? Or can God prevent earthquakes, hurricanes, and tsunamis? Good theologians are wonderers. So it's with a question that I begin this book. "Why did God create marriage?" What was God thinking about when Adam and Eve came into existence?

And while it's always a bit presumptuous for us to ask questions about God, it seems we can and we should. And to help us in our inquiry, it's best that we talk with each other about our views of God and God's creation. Shared wisdom is usually closer to the truth than when we try to figure things out all alone. In fact, among the many reasons why God became human, which was the question so brilliantly worked on by Anselm of Canterbury a thousand years ago, one conclusion is that Jesus came as a teacher of the truth about God and us. So as we seek to learn why God created marriage, we'll have to listen to what our religious tradition says as well.

I looked across the table at my wife who was quietly reading the morning paper. We were present to each other, but no words passed between us over the coffee and buttered toast. How many mornings have I begun with this same scene? Thousands? Certainly, there were too many to think about. I felt at peace, but I also knew that I was very good at denying reality. At least, that's what my wife says. She has often told me that she liked that about me, at least most of the time. Occasionally, my endearing narrowness gets on her nerves.

Over the years I have come to know that the life between wife and husband, if not the most complex of all interpersonal connections, certainly stands near the top of the list. It's almost always demanding, at times frustrating, occasionally confusing, and always a challenge. It requires strength of resolve and character, understanding and compassion, and most of all, if it is to survive, altruistic abiding love. Marriage can give one the deepest, happiest moments of life. And that's one of the reasons God created it. It was part of God's "Happiness Plan."

To use a compelling image, like skydiving, marriage may not be for everyone. But for those who have the strength and courage to marry (some would say "to answer this calling or vocation from God"), it is a wonderful way to spend one's life. I believe that, through marriage, our humanity can be wonderfully shaped into a magnificent "image of God," to use theological or spiritual language, especially during those inevitable hard times of stress and anxiety.

But having said that, I am reminded that marriage was not always thought of by society in general or the Church in particular as a sanctified and sanctifying way of life. It was not always perceived as one of God's finest ideas for humankind. On my bookshelf sits a large reference work called *Christian Spirituality*.[1] It's a hefty book of 694 pages, a compendium useful for hundreds of topics relating to the spiritual life of the Christian. Here's what it offers to married persons seeking wisdom for their spiritual life. If you look in the index under "marriage," you will find the following: "Marriage, renunciation of."

Well, we need not be discouraged. That's changing, thank God. There are now many published resources that can be quite helpful and positive supporting married life as both wonderfully human and spiritually enriching. I will be pointing to many of them in the pages ahead. Today, there's truly some good news about Christian marriage, at least from a spiritual or theological perspective. And that's where we begin our conversation in this first chapter. Now, more than ever, church leaders, theologians, spiritual writers, even poets are creating deep insights about marital life. Part of my task, as I see it, will be to summarize for you some of the supportive insights, ideas, and approaches now available to married Christians. When we have a positive interpretation of our lives,

---

[1] Frank N. Magill and Ian P. McGreal, *Christian Spirituality: The Essential Guide to the Most Influential Spiritual Writings of the Christian Tradition* (San Francisco: Harper and Row, 1988).

when we understand God's intent for marriage, we can more easily deal with difficulties. We can live with greater hope and confidence.[2]

Today's marriage scene

As mentioned in the introduction, we are going through changing and challenging times. Some of it can be quite helpful to the married; some is obviously not. For instance, there is clearly a deep valuing of interpersonal life. Maybe not everyone does, but many do. Also we now possess a rich understanding of the deep potential connection between sexuality, intimacy, and love. On the negative side, some still pay little attention to the value of marriage. I guess I could say that our culture is at best ambivalent about marriage.

My own suggestion is that it's best not to be overly fearful of the modern world and its challenges. I do not share the apocalyptic judgment that the end is near or that the world is growing more evil by the minute. By trade, I am a historical theologian, which means that I study theology and church teachings with special attention to their historical setting. Our attempts to understand many helpful truths must be filtered through the particularities and limits of the times in which their human theorists lived. This is not to say that there are not timeless truths about God and us, because I believe there are. But truth is always wrapped in and limited by the finite language and thought form in which each idea is expressed.

My historical sensitivity also reminds me over and over that there were always "Chicken Little" types warning us about falling skies and descending morals. The fact remains that we can trace the presence of evil right back to the dawn of humankind, actually to the story of Adam and Eve. There's always enough of the bad stuff around to fill the evening news and the daily newspapers. But there are also a thousand random acts of kindness filling the world each day. Sadly we don't hear enough about the positives. Further, it's important to remember that there is also the forgiving and loving presence of God, right in the middle of it all. In other words, take heart. Now is the time of your redemption and mine. Now is the moment of opportunity for great holiness, and this especially includes those of us who are married.

---

[2] See the remarkable presentation of the power of hope to assist in survival. Jerome Groopman, M.D., *The Anatomy of Hope: How People Prevail in the Face of Illness* (New York: Random House, 2004).

The Catholic Church supported this more balanced approach toward good and evil quite clearly through the documents so eloquently brought forward by the Second Vatican Council (1962–1965). I believe it's very important to engage in straightforward and balanced thinking about these matters. Maintaining a positive Christian approach to marriage is vitally important because of a historical tendency, it seems to me, to find evil and sin more in those parts of human life touching on sexuality and intimacy. Vatican II initiated a challenge to the Church to be more real, more in touch with the wonderful lives of its members. I began my career as a professional theologian during the years when the Council was in session. It has profoundly influenced my thinking, but even more to the point, it has touched my life especially as a married person. I suppose that it can be said that I am a child of Vatican II and deeply grateful to be so.

So let me share with you some of the words of that Spirit-filled gathering of church leaders that serves as background for the best thinking in the church, both when they were first written down and today as they challenge us to live fully Christian and human lives. These words come from the final document of that council. Its Latin title is most significant: *Gaudium et Spes*—Joy and Hope—the great virtues of the Christian life needed to confront today's issues, trials, and temptations. Here's what was and is written on our behalf. I've added a bit of commentary in brackets.

> The world this council has in mind is the world of women and men, the entire human family seen in its total environment. [Note the inclusive nature of this opening statement.] It is the world as the theatre of human history, bearing the marks of its travails, its triumphs and failures. [The realities of good and evil are always with us.] It is a world which Christians believe has been created and is sustained by the love of its maker [note the positive foundations for all that is], has fallen into the slavery of sin, but has been freed by Christ, who was crucified and rose again [bringing about a New Creation] in order to break the stranglehold of the evil one, so that it might be fashioned anew according to God's design and brought to its fulfillment. [The world's goodness is affirmed especially because it exists in a positive relationship to God. The world is bent in the direction of God.][3]

---

[3] Vatican II, *Gaudium et Spes* (The Pastoral Constitution on the Church in the Modern World). Quotations will be from *Vatican Council II: The Basic Sixteen Documents: Constitutions, Decrees, Declarations: A Completely Revised Translation in Inclusive Language*, ed. Austin Flannery (Northport, NY: Costello, 1996).

When we think about these words, at the whole Christian tradition for that matter, and we seek to connect it with our lives, we do theology. Theology assists us in connecting Christian faith with our daily ups and downs of life in this wonderful and very fragile world created by God. It helps us see with greater clarity what's behind the headlines and beneath the surface of our everyday experience. That's why the study of theology is often associated with developing a vision of life. The connection is extremely important for those wanting to live deeply in faith. Having a clear vision is the first step to living a deep life.

Theology, in general, has been accused of expressing itself in abstract or airy language. In my mind that's not good theology. I want to avoid that in this book about marriage. Those who do their theological thinking in the ivory towers of academia or church sometimes fail the proper task of theology, which is to provide inspiration to all humankind, give direction to those struggling along the way, while uncovering the deep presence of God beneath the surface thus awakening in us a deeper understanding and appreciation of our lives.

One of the most ancient and revered descriptions of theology was created by St. Anselm of Canterbury in the twelfth century when he described theology as "faith seeking understanding." I would add that it helps people of faith gain a greater awareness of created reality, a fuller connection between God and our lives as they are lived day by day. In a sense, Jesus often played the role of theologian by constantly pointing to what God was doing in the midst of the world, like a light on a tall mountain revealing God's somewhat hidden presence and actions in human life. For me, theology is the preeminent life science.

A Godly vision for marriage

I enjoy traveling to new places, especially outside the United States. I have been blessed with many opportunities to do this. But I always visit the local library or a favorite bookstore first to read about where I'm heading and to look at a map for indicators of what are often termed "points of interest." In a general sense, I sometimes think of myself as a tourist on this earth.

Thinking of theology as mapmaking is something I took from the writings of C. S. Lewis, the Oxford professor who did much to connect theological wisdom with ordinary life. We all know what it's like to be in a strange place with no idea of where we are. It can be a very anxious moment.

But thankfully there are maps available to us, and many are quite good. One map of Christian marriage describes it as a journey by a man and woman into the deepest parts of human interpersonal life. Upon acquiring fuller knowledge of each other (there's *always* more to learn), there follows affirmation, acceptance, and a pledge to stay together for the duration of the journey.

That's at the basis of the promise made at the time of the wedding: to remain together whatever happens. It's a daring statement. Some would say it's an almost irrational promise. Many might note, for instance, that people change. New circumstances arise. There is a whole cartload of "what ifs" that can challenge those making such bold promises to each other. But that's the greatness of Christian marriage. Its claims defy calculation and assessment. Once made, the promise to be with and for each other travels ahead in time defying much of the so-called wisdom of the world. This is especially so when the promise stretches to the whole of life and includes in its formulation the condition of "for better or for worse." It's always worthwhile to think about what a courageous act marriage can be.

Now here's where some theological wisdom can enrich and enlighten this mix. I like to think that theology helps us connect heaven with earth, God's ways with our own. That's what God wants marriage to be: a grand mimicking of perfection.

Marriage, for example, is about unconditional commitment. The question is: where else does this sort of thing happen? Well, if you think about it, with God and us! That's the underlying theme of the message of Jesus. God stays with us, loving us so much that even when we stray off the path, God is there to pull us back. God's love is not like ours because it exceeds ours in intent, intensity, and perseverance. Nevertheless, we are gracefully equipped to do a good job of imitation. And that's what we do in Christian marriage. We attempt to seed into marital love some semblance of God's love. Certainly the thought of John Paul II was based on this idea. No other pope ever said or wrote so much about Christian marriage as did this pope. When connecting the salvific work of Jesus with the life of the married, he wrote the following, "the marriage of baptized persons thus becomes a real symbol of the new and eternal covenant sanctioned in the blood of Christ."[4]

We do the work of Jesus in many kinds of social settings. It's not just in marriage. But in marriage many of us obviously fall short of this

---

[4] John Paul II, *Familiaris Consortio* (On the Family) sec. 13.

exalted challenge. Too often we settle conflict with violence. We solve problems by running out the back door. We fail to communicate. At times, we don't even want to! This is not by any stretch of the imagination unconditional love.

But there are moments when the barrier between earth and heaven falls away. And nothing does this more effectively than when we act in ways that are genuinely kind, altruistic, and loving. Christian marriage is one of those instances where "symbolically" this happens. Now, before going on, I must say something about symbols because this use of language is often misunderstood.

Symbols participate in the reality they signify. Symbols connect with the reality expressed. For instance, smoke is a symbol of fire. A kiss is a symbol of affection. A smile symbolizes a positive inner disposition. Symbols can be fraudulent or fake. A political candidate shakes hands with every passerby. Is that handshake a symbol of genuine connection and concern? We all know the answer. It depends on the candidate. So symbols can be real or fake. Most people are quite able to know the difference. Teenagers seem especially adept at identifying fake symbols. Nothing is worse for them than "a fake." It violates their basic order of reality. They are quite correct in their judgment.

But there are good symbols, and Christian marriage lived day after day is one of the best.

In the history of theology, there's a most interesting text relating to the use of marriage as a symbol of the love between man and woman. In the Bible, it's called The Canticle of Canticles or Song of Solomon or Song of Songs. It's filled with wonderful love poetry that seems to describe the love between a husband and wife. And current biblical scholars agree that these songs were often sung at wedding feasts, which, for the record, were rather wild and lengthy celebrations in the time of Jesus and before. Here's where it gets interesting.

The language and images in The Canticle of Canticles are borderline erotic. Read it and you'll see. Maybe that's why we rarely hear it read in church. Now you might have heard that for many centuries the Catholic Church was not quite comfortable with the physical side of human sexuality. So when Christian theologians of the first millennium commented on this book of the Bible, they labeled it as allegorical. What that means is that its literal meaning was not its true meaning. It was like "code language" pointing to something secret and mysterious like God's love for us. This was correct except the commentators skipped a step. They failed to acknowledge the symbolic sacredness of marital love that was, of course, quite sexual.

Two clear examples of a nonsexual interpretation of this biblical book would be Origen (185–254) who wrote ten volumes of commentary without once referring to real marriage. His spirit of understanding was pretty much followed by Bernard of Clairvaux (1090–1153) who composed and published eighty-six sermons on this book again seeing nothing in it that was connected with the human. It was all about God.[5]

We can even read of how the church of that era valued marriage without intimate sexual relations, the so-called Joseph and Mary marriage, as an ideal. My guess is that two thought currents were operative at that time. First, there was great reverence for the life of consecrated virginity. Those who pursued such a life were considered the direct descendants of the early martyrs of the church. So the closer one came to being a dedicated virgin in God's kingdom, the closer one was to God.

Second, as we learn more about the typical marriage of those days, the more we realize that it was not a life of love and freely-chosen service, but more one of servitude to the demands of the extended family. We will look without success to find in the literature of that time the words "marriage" and "love" in the same sentence. The fact was that most marriages, especially among those with some economic status, were prearranged by families who used such unions for their own gain. Progeny was also important as a means of securing long title to land and other economic resources. We would hope that a certain amount of love became part of the marriages of those times, and perhaps it did. But that's not what marriage was for. In fact, the close association that we make today between love and marriage is a rather recent phenomenon.[6]

In no way do I want this to sound as if the church did not value marriage. But as late as 1917, the church was still using the language that the primary purpose of marriage was the procreation and education of children. It was not until Vatican II that the wonderful love language of our faith was woven into the description of marriage.

Many people are surprised to learn that when the church finally and officially listed its seven sacraments at the Council of Trent in the sixteenth century, it was marriage that was the final sacrament to make the cut. In previous centuries, various theologians included marriage in

---

[5] To see how much the church has used the Song of Songs as an allegory of God's love, see the four volumes of *Bernard of Clairvaux on the Song of Songs* (Kalamazoo, MI: Cistercian Publications, 1983, 1980, 1979, 1971).

[6] See Stephanie Coontz, *Marriage, A History: From Obedience to Intimacy, or How Love Conquered Marriage* (New York: Viking, 2005).

their own personal accounting of the sacraments, but their opinions did not have the weight of being considered official church teaching.

It's also interesting that two other rituals were also considered as possible sacraments. One was the coronation of kings, which for years was closely related to the life of the church, and a theology developed that supported a so-called divine right given to proper regal authority. The other ritual vying for consideration as a sacrament was religious profession. Eventually it was argued that religious vows were more an extension of baptism so they didn't "need" further sacramental identity. Religious profession was described at times as a second baptism.

It's worthwhile to reflect on why marriage came to become an official sacrament of the church. I would like to think that it had something to do with the life and witness of ordinary Christians who were married. Their experience of married love gave to them some inkling or sense of God's love. Refer back to what I mentioned about symbol. Genuine symbolism participates in the reality it symbolizes.

Using good maps

While no one has kept a daily journal describing how the Christian map of marriage changed, we have the hindsight of historical investigation to help us view this happening. There are two sections of the Bible that alert us to this discovery. The first is found in the book of Hosea.

There, the prophet's own life becomes a kind of parable or symbol of God's relationship with Israel. He had married a rather spirited woman whose name was Gomer. Apparently her life with Hosea left her with some kind of an unsatisfied hunger so she went off to the local Canaanite hill shrines for additional excitement. Now these "places of worship" were not your typical sacred gathering place, although the Canaanites claimed they were. Their religion was especially focused on achieving fertility both of the land and of humankind. In other words, Gomer was most likely engaged in hilltop fertility rites which were forbidden to God's chosen people. We don't know how it went for her, but we do know she returned to Hosea asking for reentry into his life. Here's where the symbolism comes in. God invites him to take Gomer back, forgive the trespasses she did, and start their marriage once again. The symbolism refers to the fact that what happened in Hosea's marriage also happened to the Israelites in general. Once connected to God, they left their religious practices and went off to the hills, much like Gomer. God wanted to show through the marriage of Hosea that God could and would forgive.

The second instance where the Bible compared God's covenant with the people and marriage occurs in chapter five of the Epistle to the Ephesians. Once again, a parallel is drawn between human marriage and divine covenant. The author is describing Christian marriage and states the following. "This [marriage] is a great mystery, and I am applying it to Christ and the church."[7]

Slowly marital symbolism crept into the consciousness of the church. The use of the word "mystery" played an important role in the church's recognition of Christian marriage as sacramental because it was the Greek word for "sacrament." But I think it would take more than biblical passages to bring the church to its positive portrayal of marriage. It had to overcome a couple of obstacles like the fact that marriage included sexual relations, which the church mostly failed to appreciate as holy and good during most of its early years. Also, marriage was clearly something that was part of creation. It went all the way back to the Garden of Eden. The other sacraments of the church, like Eucharist and Baptism, came from the ministry of Jesus. And while St. John's Gospel has that wonderful account of Jesus attending the wedding feast at Cana, there is no indication that he "instituted" a sacrament there. Mostly we see him extending the party in a rather miraculous way. Biblical scholars would say that the passage is symbolic, but not about marriage. It's symbolic rather of the beginning of God's kingdom with a great banquet, a favorite image in the Bible.

Let's summarize. The Christian map of marriage was officially redrawn at the Council of Trent in the sixteenth century. The idea of sanctity in marriage has been advanced in more recent times with some of this awareness being captured in Vatican II and subsequent papal writings. As I have suggested, the experience of married Christians also had a role to play in this "discovery" of sanctity and holiness in marriage. Like all historical changes, however, this revision, as we are calling it, took time. In fact, the shift in awareness and appreciation is still happening.

Part of this change happens as we more fully connect our interpersonal lives with our life with God. The New Testament has Jesus saying that the two great commandments, love of God and love of neighbor, are really one commandment. We love God in and through our neighbor.

---

[7] Eph 5:32 (NRSV).

John's first epistle boldly states that if we say we love God and don't also love our neighbor, we're liars. You can't get much clearer than that.

I would also add that the treasure of experiencing God's love in and through marital love was always there. But it was more like a buried treasure. It required discovery at a personal level and at a communal level. Christianity is basically about God's love shining forth in the life of Christ. Jesus was God's living word in our midst. His love was so great that he gave his life for us. Imitation of that love is at the core of Christian belief and life. As our appreciation of the presence and power of love deepens, so too will our theology of marriage.[8]

But this orientation of neighbor love does not come easily in a culture so geared to serving the desires and needs of the individual person. It's a very long journey from an over-stimulated ego to a sensitive relational self. The flow of contemporary life goes in the other direction. Popular culture says put yourself as number one. Your needs should be placed before those of anyone else. In the next chapter we will talk about the complexities of love, so here we will simply mention that it must possess some sense of altruism. While healthy love of self remains important, our love journey must leave the privacy of self-centered concerns and reach outside to others. And even then we have to be careful that we don't fall into a false orientation.

I recall a statement that captures this illusionary love quite well. It was: "I need you to be me." Taken literally that turns the other person into a means of my own selfish pursuit of identity. The other is simply a function in my life. Martin Buber would say this is not a genuine I-Thou relationship but one of an I-it kind. In that sense, it is not truly interpersonal, but rather a using of the other for my own needs. Pope John II described this as a demeaning of the person, a loss of genuine human life.

Interpersonal awareness is another aspect of living that may not come easy. We have to "get into the shoes" of the other, see the world through the eyes of another. It's akin to leaving oneself or better, a stretching of oneself into the personhood of the other. We transcend all stereotypes and role descriptions when we do this. It's just me and you and that is enough. I believe that people are capable of this, but it requires a certain level of receptivity and listening, an openness to hear the word of the other, an expansion of mindfulness to include a reality completely unique and different from oneself.

---

[8] See Michael St. Clair, *Human Relationships and the Experience of God: Object Relations and Religion* (Mahwah, NJ: Paulist Press, 1994).

Christian marriage is deeply interpersonal in that sense. Because it is so deeply interpersonal, every instance of the sacrament of Christian marriage is quite unique. That's because of another wonderful feature of the theology of marriage. The true ministers of this sacrament are not the priest or the deacon (they serve as the official church witness to the exchange of vows) but the couple themselves. The wife administers this sacrament to her husband and he does the same for her. Later on in this book I will add that the sacramental life of marriage is not just "given" at the time of the wedding, but it is an ongoing possibility, a genuine reality in their life together. That means couples can be administering this sacrament, to use some rather formal church language, time after time. It's helpful also to think of marriage as a special kind of friendship and, therefore, it has some of the same dynamics as does friendship, a privileged aspect of life.[9]

Further, because the basic material of this sacrament is interpersonal and each person and couple is unique, these new sacramental events are as varied as are the peculiarities of each married couple. In other words, there's no one way. I make this point for two reasons. One, we are a culture of copiers. We like to imagine ourselves as superstars and winners. Maybe that's an ancient need because these archetypes have served many cultures and embody certain idealized forms. The point is that each of us is not always comfortable in being ourselves. We imitate. Second, the church itself often uses the language of imitation. We are called to imitate Christ or Mary, his mother, or one of the saints. Certainly this imitation is not to be taken simplistically. Such directive is a call to imitate their faith, their love for others, their goodness.

A few years ago I was addressing a large gathering of married couples on the topic of the sacrament of Christian marriage. I made the point of uniqueness and that each could co-create their own sacramental expression of marriage. I wasn't arguing that anything goes and that there are no guidelines or rules for Christian marriage. I simply wanted people to feel their uniqueness as they contribute their own gifts to their marriage. After my presentation a couple came up to me in tears. My first inclination was to think that I presented so poorly that I drove some of my listeners to tears. Fortunately for me, I was able to quickly interpret their tears as joyful. They said that for a long time they had felt inferior as a married couple. They had friends who were very affectionate, who

---

[9] An excellent theological work that uses friendship as a basic model for understanding the sacramental dimension of life is Bernard Cooke, *Sacraments and Sacramentality*, 2nd ed. (Mystic, CT: Twenty-Third Publications, 1994).

spoke openly about their marriages and had no difficulty expressing their feelings for each other in public. The couple before me was quiet and reserved. Their feelings of inferiority arose from their not being like the others. They told me that my words gave them the assurance that they were okay even though they were a little different from their friends. Good for them, I thought. It's always satisfying to realize that one's words are helpful, especially when I felt the principle of sacramental distinctiveness applied so well to Christian marriage.

Staying on the map

Catholic theology is a rich blend of basic beliefs from the Bible and from the tradition of the Catholic Church extending all the way back to Jesus. It is captured in creeds, teachings from church councils, and the writings of popes and respected Catholic theologians. Theology is very much a living and dynamic project expressing the richness of the church's intellectual tradition. It is ultimately founded on the church's acceptance of divine revelation especially through the life and teachings of Jesus Christ, God's Word made manifest in human history.

Theology will also bear the imprint of those professionally committed to this ministry. In recent years it has been enriched and blessed especially by the contributions of lay men and women as well as theologians from non-Western countries. Making theology an inclusive venture is critical to assuring ourselves that we have the means to fully reflect on God's word for today.

The theology of Christian marriage has greatly profited from dialogue and writings stimulated by the insights encapsulated in the documents of Vatican II. Since then, this theology has become more personal, pastoral, and practical—qualities certainly welcomed by the married and those who minister with them.

The theological map of Christian marriage may appear more like an adventure map or one that notes all the scenic side trips rather than a simple map starting at point A and going directly to point B. That's because of what I have already mentioned about the uniqueness of every marriage. But its uniqueness doesn't imply that the couple wanders aimlessly on a personal spiritual journey.

We have already noted that it is, first of all, a journey specified by the love between them. It also demands the human qualities of freedom, responsibility, and openness to learn from God's Spirit particularly as that Spirit communicates through the teachings of the church. But I have to add that these teachings are meant to liberate and support marriage so that it can reach its full potential before God and before the rest of the world. Sometimes we think of rules or directives as only confining or restricting, rather than freeing and being there for our own betterment. Jesus said that the truth will make us free and this applies directly to our holy lives as married couples. The truth about love and commitment that Jesus proclaimed is "good news" to those who seek with an open and honest heart the best life imaginable.

Included in a theology of marriage for our times must be a discussion of the equality between the sexes. Here we listen to the wise and penetrating assessment of women theologians who have pointed to deeply-seated prejudices and unjust structures in society that have almost a timeless beginning. Today we are trying to rectify past violations of women's rights especially as they connect with the social institution of marriage. With marriage being primarily a relationship between the sexes at the most personal level of all, it is incumbent that all social ills touching their relationship be named and corrected. This will be a lifelong challenge in each marriage.

Another area of pressing concern has to do with the procreative or generative side of marriage. We have already noted a cultural danger that invites us to pursue our own private goals without serious consideration of others. This is no small matter because marriage was not intended by God as "private property" or a relationship that is to be used simply to fulfill individual needs. There is more to marriage than just the couple. Christian marital love is to extend outward from the couple. For most, this will mean procreation of new life. Such love is founded on expressions of love that are rooted in the teachings of the church relating to responsible parenthood. But the generative love of the couple will also be responsive to the needs of others outside the immediate family. It may involve care of aging parents or other family members. It might include caring for foster children. It might entail the adoption of children. In recent years, generous couples have gone to the far reaches of the world seeking orphaned or abandoned children in great need.

Generous marital love seeks opportunities to serve the needs of the world outside the home. Again, this outreach may feel somewhat countercultural when the home is felt more to be a fortress than a place where strangers can find a welcoming hand.

When Jesus addressed the topic of marriage, his disciples thought that his view seemed overly demanding. During his time, marriage was in somewhat of an unhealthy state. Divorce and separation were commonly based on the will of the husband. Jesus lived in a patriarchal society. Women were often thought of in the family as the man's property. So were children, slaves, and animals. In many ways, Jesus supported the dignity and rights of all. He called for lifelong marital fidelity and commitment. When his disciples questioned him on this, he agreed that it was a challenge but said that God's presence and assistance would be available. The need for divine assistance was needed both then and now. He laid down some basics: the equality of all, the importance of deep, altruistic love, the importance of children, respect for the body, and the importance of giving thanks and celebrating God's gifts.

He gave us a good start in understanding why God created marriage. Marriage is filled with deep human and religious meaning. Recall it being described as a mystery in the Epistle to the Ephesians. Mystery, in the biblical sense, does not mean it's like a mystery novel. Mystery means that the reality pointed to has roots so deep that they extend into the person of God. When something is mysterious in that sense, God can be touched in some way if we go deep enough into the reality. In a sense, all God's creation is a mystery. Marriage is one of the best places to find it.

Astronomers and other scientists often say the deeper they enter the reality they are observing, the closer they feel to seeing the hand of God. Many claim to sense something of God when seeing the wonders of nature, like a beautiful sunset over the ocean or the fury of waves smashing against a rocky coastline. Both the storms and the calm of nature can carry questioning observers into a depth of perception that defies ordinary surface observation.

It also seems that some parts of created reality more easily allow us deeper than usual entrance into their secret depths. Celtic spirituality speaks of places in creation where the barrier between earth and heaven, the created and the Creator, are thin. In those places, the divine can seem close at hand. I believe a marriage, seasoned with deep love, is one of those "thin" places. As the biblical text just mentioned notes, marriage can symbolize and embody the relation between God and us, between Christ and the church.

Vatican II described Christian marriage as "the intimate partnership of life and the love which constitutes" it.[10] The interconnection of life with love mirrors the most basic act of God creating our universe. God loves, and life comes into existence. When this happens in marriage, one could say that God is close by, or better, part of this event. The New

---

[10] Vatican II, *Gaudium et Spes*, 48.

Testament names God as Love. The essence of God is to love. So too is the essence of Christian marriage. No wonder Christian marriage is characterized as a great mystery within Christian faith.

It has taken most of the lifetime of the church to come to a clear description and definition of marriage that incorporates marital love at its core. But it's also worth remembering that connecting deep human love with marriage was late in appearing in general human history. Mostly, marriage in past times served to meet the needs of the larger family unit, the clan, the tribe, or the state. Love between husband and wife would be welcomed, but not required. Plus, the full demands of deep, altruistic, and generous love are not easy. Of course, anyone observing the dynamics of contemporary marriage will recognize this. Marital love invites our fuller attention and understanding and we will explore this in the next chapter.

Chapter Two

Why is love so important?

For most of human history, marriage was not directly connected with the love between the husband and wife. Marriage was usually arranged by parents for many different reasons. Some were economic. It was a great way to pick up more land. Some were political. Why fight with your neighbor if you could share grandchildren? Some were personal. He wanted good food and she wanted protection. Besides, they both wanted legitimate children. Doesn't sound very romantic, does it? Nevertheless that was the way it was for hundreds, if not thousands, of years.

Today, of course, we understand marriage as based primarily on the love between a woman and a man. So the first important thing to say about Christian marriage in our time is that it's an interpersonal relationship created and sustained by the energy generated by mutual love. Each person's love for one another goes both ways, back and forth, from day to day, even minute by minute. Their love for each other energizes them, deepens and expands their humanity, and sanctifies them as persons before God.

But after affirming this important fact, I must note right away that we must put on the table an important issue concerning our emphasis on marital love. The idea of love is one of the slipperiest concepts we have. We like to imagine love between persons as mature, open-ended, and lasting a lifetime. Jesus was not afraid to call love the foundation of just about everything he stood for, including the way he lived and died. His life was filled with love for everyone.

So one of the first challenges we face in our understanding of marriage is to be specific about what we mean by love as the basis of marriage. In our contemporary world, love is often equated with romantic feelings. If love becomes frozen at that level, its power for the good of both persons is seriously diminished. Romantic love can be quite self-centered and be nothing much more than feelings.[1]

A recent study of love in America notes that our culture contains a wide variety of ideas about the nature of love. People select those ideas or approaches that best suit their interests, needs, and experiences. This amalgam of ideas about love, to use an image in that study, is like a huge toolbox whose contents can be used in whatever way seems best in the circumstances. If some of these ideas are contradictory, like when love is described as outside human control and that love is primarily a matter of free choice and decision-making, so be it. Our cultural toolbox is simply a container. There's something for everyone.[2]

But, as I have already noted, our map of Christian marriage, while connected with the culture, in a sense, goes beyond it. Its wisdom comes partly from God, the source of deeper truth. It is rooted in the teachings of Jesus. For him love was a strong and powerful concept. It was the core energy that created deeds of generosity and compassion. Love is how Jesus explained his death, as well as all those moments leading up to it. Love is also the foundation of Christ's resurrection as God's Spirit continues to be present to us and love us. Although love can be misunderstood, manipulated, and misdirected, it's still the best foundation we have for the kind of relationship God intended marriage to be.

John Paul II had spoken and written more about marriage and family life than all the previous popes combined. As an ordinary parish priest he assisted young couples in preparing for marriage. As a university professor, he often attended to issues facing the young both before and after they were married. And as pope, the first major international meeting of bishops he presided over was on the topic of marriage and family life.

Most recall well his appeal to the young of the world and the chant that became famous when he appeared before them. The crowds of young people would chant, "John Paul II, we love you." And after a wry smile, he'd say back to them, "John Paul II, he loves you." He never tired of reminding them and us that ours was a vocation to love, whether married or not.

---

[1] One of the strongest arguments against this tendency is in David M. McCarthy, *Sex and Love in the Home: A Theology of the Household* (London: SCM Press, 2001).

[2] See Ann Swidler, *Talk of Love: How Culture Matters* (Chicago: The University of Chicago Press, 2001).

After that first meeting with bishops, he wrote a lengthy document on marriage and family life in today's world. Here's a passage which typified the spirit not only of this document, but of his lengthy papacy. "God is love and in himself he lives a mystery of personal loving communion. Creating the human race in his own image and continually keeping it in being, God inscribed in the humanity of man and woman the vocation, and thus the capacity and responsibility of love and communion. Love is therefore the fundamental and innate vocation of every human being."[3]

Love in God's world

Love is central to human existence because in a very deep sense, we exist because God loves each of us. And our returning love to God, and to all that's of God, is our proper response to this unfathomable reality. God's love for us is to be read as the first line in the story of our existence. Our loving response is line two. Each one of us was ushered into existence because God loved us into life. In this way, and only in this way, did we come into being. This is sometimes a difficult idea to accept, given the often complex and perplexing nature of human existence. We all experience our existence as ambiguous at times, often frustrating, filled with suffering, saturated with difficulties, and finally ending in inevitable death. Are these expressions of a loving God? It takes courageous faith to answer in the affirmative and to remain hopeful in the midst of inescapable hard times.

Nevertheless, it's important to keep a sense of God's love at the foundation of all reality. Creation is a divine gift. So too is our personal existence. And as I present a Christian view of marriage, I hope to show that this understanding of life is especially germane for those who are married. Married life incorporates one very important and distinct way we respond to being loved by God. Christian marital love is a distinctive attempt to love as God loves. It includes an unconditional aspect as much as this is humanly possible. Christian marriage can become a powerful symbol of divine love in human form. It can be God's love incorporated and made real in human form. The Epistle to the Ephesians gives witness to this deep dimension of "breakthrough."

[3] John Paul II, On the Family, 11.

Even when describing love in a Christian context, we are not "out of the woods" when it comes to possible distortions. In marriage, for instance, there is a long tradition of "spiritualizing" love. Some would say that dualism, the separating of body from the soul, the physical from the spiritual, is one of the great heresies of Christianity.[4] Because Christianity almost came to the point of disdaining bodily love, we often forget that marital love includes physical, sensual, and corporeal dimensions of life. And those expressions, while wonderfully inclusive of personal sexuality, extend to the whole of the physical side of relating to each other. Gestures of kindness and generosity in physically working hard for and with each other, in physically caring for each other especially during times of illness or injury, in maintaining a common home, in the labor required "in making a living," in all the bodily things required in caring for children, yes, in all these acts, the love between wife and husband is articulated.

Another danger of misinterpretation comes through turning religious and marital responses into sentimentality. Generally this means that emotions are exaggerated, and reason and common sense are blocked or ignored. Occasionally, I like to watch afternoon soap operas because that genre is so good at portraying runaway sentimentality. Every event drips with emotion. The musical background intensifies feelings of loss, rejection, attraction, fear—hardly any emotion is overlooked in any episode. I know these programs provide many with a welcome diversion from their daily lives, but I would hope that no one would believe that they are honest portrayals of life, much less idealized versions of what should be. Nevertheless they are good examples of a certain approach to life and love.

Religion also slips into currents of exaggerated emotion. Certain preaching styles play on human emotions. What's called devotional life can also fall off the edge of reasonable faith into a well of syrupy feelings. The media love to take note of these moments of "religious fervor." It makes for good copy. Oftentimes they also use such scenes as a negative critique of religion and all those who practice it.

When religion is connected with interpersonal relationships, you can have an explosive mix that can energize marriage or be a disservice to its best interests. Emotion is a major part of healthy human life and love. But just as this love can be too spiritual, it can also be too emotional.

---

[4] Daniel J. O'Leary, *Lost Souls: The Catholic Church Today* (Dublin: Columba Press, 1999) 29.

Marriage should be a freeing experience that brings forth the fullness of human loving response. Christianity is about being fully alive and not straightjacketed into some narrow version of interpersonal slavery. Again, we have to note a cultural distortion around all the folk wisdom saying in a thousand ways that once you marry, your happy and full life as a person is basically over. I would hope that it would be just the opposite.

Of course, the world is a challenging mix of grace and sin, human weakness and human glory. But the entrance of sin into our world need not be viewed as some kind of total destruction of the human person or society. One of the many fine qualities of Catholic thought is the affirmation that while our human nature was wounded by sin, it was not destroyed.

Further, the work begun in Christ was one of restoration and re-building. As St. Paul wrote, we are to glorify God in our bodies. I take this to mean that the results of the Incarnation and Resurrection of Christ work their way into the deepest recesses of our humanity. Grace affects everything, or to use the language of medieval theology, grace perfects nature. The Christian message includes a fully positive and all-inclusive view of marital love. There is a great and glorious fit between Christian faith and marriage.

Loving the nearest neighbor

There is a very reliable test of our love of God. It's called love of neighbor. Most Christians know this. It's in the New Testament. It's been preached in our liturgies. It's been written about in our documents. And it's lived out by countless Christians throughout the world. Concrete love of neighbor is not just a good idea; it informs a way of life where we actively seek ways to help others in need, near and far.

Again, we face an important question: "Do we willingly help the distant neighbor, but overlook the person right at hand?" As a wonderful reminder of keeping a focus on all our neighbor's needs, I strongly favor the inclusion in the Mass of the ancient kiss or exchange of peace. I have read criticisms of this practice by those who claim that it distracts from the sacredness of the liturgy. I believe that I stand on firm ground in proposing that this acknowledgment of neighbor right next to us is at the heart of all that is sacred. God is present in the close neighbor and, especially as Mother Teresa so often noted, in those most in need.

Of course, "need" is a word apropos to many situations. We can easily recognize need in the hungry, the homeless, and the sick. It's clearly apparent. But what about the need of the lonely for a kind word, the need for recognition by the overlooked, the need for understanding by the misunderstood, or the need for touch by those so often ignored? These are real needs and those who genuinely love recognize these kinds of needs. They see it where others miss it. They respond to it when others walk away. And it is no exaggeration to say that one of the worst places to feel these less apparent forms of need is in a marriage.

I know a marriage therapist who begins working with a couple with a survey of each one's unmet needs. She knows something quite crucial about interpersonal life and how it works. Research has shown that when needs are not met at home, people will search for help elsewhere. This is not to say that marital life will fulfill all personal needs. That's unrealistic and even dangerous to hope for this. But, yes, marriage should fulfill basic interpersonal needs. To add a practical suggestion here, there's nothing wrong with a person expressing unmet needs. Men especially can get into the role of the stalwart warrior and claim that they do not need help from anyone. They are strong and totally self-sufficient. They claim that an unmet need is a sign of weakness. They are wrong in this judgment. It's not a sign of weakness to ask for help. That's simply acknowledging that one is human!

So we do well to note that both the Jewish and Christian traditions speak clearly and strongly about love of neighbor. Neighbor could be simply defined as those who share our human condition. They can be near or far. It's also important to be as inclusive as possible in recognizing the neighbor in all situations. This includes loving both the stranger and the one that most likely shocked those who first heard Jesus say this, the enemy!

And we are also invited to express our love of neighbor in thoughts, words, and deeds, to use a traditional formula that I learned originally applied to sin. But these are also ways we love. So a first point for consideration for those of us who are married would be to ask how often we keep each other present in our thoughts, in our concerns, in our worries, in our desires, and in our hopes for the future. I like to recall what St. Thomas Aquinas wrote about love where he described its essence being the *desire* of the lover that the beloved live and live well.[5] I am reminded of married soldiers in battle who keep going in very trying

---

[5] Thomas Aquinas, *Summa Theologiae*, II, II, 25, 7.

circumstances with only the thought that some day they will be united to their wives or husbands.

Loving words and other gestures of affection are also important. Language takes loving thoughts and feelings from inside and brings them to the outside so they can be known and shared. Good words nourish and enrich us. They can make all the difference between darkness and light in a relationship. They clear up ambiguity and add an ever-deepening sense of being loved. Expressing loving words, I also believe, serves as a kind of fuel increasing love. We have an annual celebration of love. More chocolates and more flowers are sold that day than any other. While parts of the annual celebration of Valentine's Day bother me, I am fully supportive of its basic intent which is to celebrate love. I am also reminded that the feast was originally created in memory of two saints, both named Valentinus, who were martyrs for their Christian faith. They gave their lives for God and for others. They loved without limit.

Finally, we come to the important issue that love of neighbor must be expressed in deed and that its deeds truly serve and help the one loved. Many will recall the Broadway music lyric that goes something like, "if you say you love me, show me!" Too readily some people talk a good game of love but do nothing to show their love. They don't walk their talk.

Philosophers call this extending of one's life and energy for another the self-transcendent dimension of love. When we authentically love, all aspects of a "me-first" orientation slip away as we reach across the chasm between us to connect. This emphasis on *action* on behalf of others can be found in the writings of John Paul II written even before he became pope.[6] And surely his being a pope of action was apparent right until he breathed his last.

Toward the end of the Gospel of Matthew we find the stirring account of the Last Judgment told in remarkable detail.[7] Those who were judged to be on the side of God, fed the hungry, gave drink to the thirsty, welcomed the stranger, clothed the naked, cared for the sick, and visited those in prison. What all these examples share is that someone was in need and something specific could be done to help them. Those who responded with assistance were saved. Those who didn't, weren't.

---

[6] Karol Wojtyla, *The Acting Person*, trans. Andrzej Potocki (Boston: D. Reidel Publishing Co., 1979).

[7] Matt 25:31-46.

Most people interpret this story as referring to the Last Judgment, our final moment of accountability before God. Given the richness of the Jesus story, we can easily imagine a large courtroom or a vast field where all are assembled. Then the sorting takes place with some placed on God's good side and others somewhere else.

But I have another way of interpreting this judgment because I believe that it happens well before the so-called final day. It applies to that moment in time when the act of love is done or left undone. In that moment we receive a judgment that directly touches our humanity. It's an application of a phrase I treasure: love creates life.

It is my deep conviction that our existence is fluid and open to change. Some would call this "transformation." The change can contribute to our betterment or our being made less. I don't question the basic dignity we enjoy as persons and the rights and responsibilities that flow directly from that. What I am referring to here is a certain quality of our personhood. It is part of the abundant life described by Jesus that he came to give us, or more appropriately, that he came to give us the *opportunity* to achieve. God's call and assistance are given at literally every moment of our life. We can respond positively or turn our back to these sacred opportunities.

We confess at Mass for all our failings through what we have done or failed to do. Traditional moral teaching calls these sins of commission and sins of omission. Most will say that the latter category of omission covers much more than what we have done. However one fills in the blanks, it amounts to thousands of moments. We literally construct our humanity and the condition of the whole world, act by act, moment by moment, good deed by good deed. Nothing is unaccounted for.

That's why I like the judgment metaphor in Matthew's Gospel. And I like its application to ordinary acts of helping others. The application to married life and love should be apparent. The moral dimensions of marriage are as extensive as is the life shared by the couple. And it includes everything. I say this not to create guilt, but to create an awareness of the full realm of possible personal and relational growth that partners can experience in marriage.

The contours of marital love

The commandment to love one's neighbor is universal. It challenges all of us, whatever our life condition might be. Every state in life, every sacred vocation has its challenges, its reward, and its contours. Here I will attend to Christian marriage.

When we marry, we specify that our spouse will play a central role in the ensuing drama of our life. We determine through promises, freely given and freely shared, that this is a lifelong commitment. As a married couple, we will walk the path of life hand in hand, sharing good days and those not so good, combining our energy, our hearts, our concerns, our dreams, literally all that we are and all that we have. We will offer the gift of ourselves for one another. This is a very challenging way to live. That some pull back from or seriously fear such a commitment is understandable. As I mentioned already, it's not for everyone.

As married persons, we chose to be primary neighbors for each other. We will each most likely have many "outside interests" but they are all to be factored into the marriage relationship. Christian marriage does not imply that we think alike, have similar personalities, or that we do everything together. Marriage is a joining of two persons that, for starters, are different from each other by every cell in their bodies. Embracing a loving person different from ourselves has its own challenges. I sometimes think that marriage entails an application of what I noted in Matthew's Gospel as "welcoming the stranger." In many ways men and women are "strangers" to each other because of their deep and pervasive differences.

In a society that is tending, I believe, to homogenize the genders, I think we have to go back to some baseline thinking about differences between the genders that I think of as partly God-given. I am not about to list the many differences because such naming may be impossible, especially when addressing the deeper parts of the person. I am also quite aware that earlier attempts to designate attributes or qualities of each gender often fell into the pit of stereotyping or of rating one gender over another. Sometimes this was subtle, sometimes it was blatant.

I prefer an approach that focuses on finding out what these differences are within each particular marriage. Personal qualities are usually a complex mixture of nature and nurture. Accepting that means that universalizing is an activity to be questioned from the start. How I embody masculinity and how my wife embodies femininity will be unique in many ways. Generalization can be helpful as a starting point for observation, analysis, and conversation. But it's worth remembering that we are not things or simply members of a species. It takes a lifetime to fully know another person. One of the more recent methods used to meet potential marriage partners is to "shop" via the Internet. Many sites show people's pictures, bodily dimensions, education, and interests as a prelude to an eventual first meeting. I see nothing inherently wrong with this. But we need to recognize that this is but a first step. Good marriage preparation must include getting to know any potential spouse as fully as possible. We are each unique persons. And the substance of that uniqueness is what forms the center of our deep coming together in marriage.

Because of the influence in both society and in religion of the biblical description concerning the creation of man and woman, I want to say a few words about that description. It's helpful for us even though our culture differs quite a bit from the culture in which this description was created. Biblical scholars tell us that passages like this are both descriptive and proscriptive. They present biblical ideals, some of which are timeless.

First of all, we note that it was written in a culture of powerful masculine dominance, where patrilineal connections structured all society. Husbands and fathers of those times listed their possessions as the land and buildings they owned, and all that was in or on them. This included their farm animals and implements, their slaves, their wives, and their children. And over all of them, the man exercised absolute lordship and control. Yet the creation account in Genesis provides a very different view.

After mentioning that it was not good for the man to be alone, God created a suitable partner for him.

So the Lord God caused a deep sleep to fall upon the man, and he slept;
then he took one of his ribs and closed up its place with flesh.
And the rib that the Lord God had taken from the man he made into a woman
and brought her to the man. Then the man said,
"This at last is bone of my bones
and flesh of my flesh;
this one shall be called Woman,
for out of Man this one was taken."
Therefore a man leaves his father and his mother
and clings to his wife, and they become one flesh.
And the man and his wife were both naked,
and were not ashamed.[8]

[8] Gen 2:21-25.

Two important points can be made from this poetic and richly symbolic account of creation. First, man and woman were made of the same raw material. Both were flesh and bone which we can interpret as having a sturdy foundation but also a soft side as well. Some commentators note that God's taking the man's rib implies taking a part of him that is close to his heart. The heart in Hebrew lore was the center of human life, the reservoir of what was deeply important to each person. We recall the words of Jesus where he said that where one's heart was, there we'd find the person's treasure. Therefore, we can see in the passage an affirmation of similarity between man and woman and also some appreciation of the closeness God intends between them.

The second point I would make comes from the last verse, the one about leaving mother and father and clinging to each other and becoming one flesh. This seems to be presented almost as if it were obvious. But would it have been in the culture in which such a description was first composed? Hardly! Leaving parents to form a new and separate social unit was considered unheard of. Today it's different. If most children don't freely leave the parental home by a certain age, especially if they are married, they are ushered out. But that's not how it always was. In fact, the creation of what we call the nuclear family is a rather modern invention. Hebrew life back then was structured around what we call the multigenerational extended family. Nevertheless, there it is in black and white. Leave home. Set up your own family. Whether it actually meant geographical departure is not clear. What is clear is the creation of something new and valuable in its own right.

Two in one flesh could mean a lot of things. The original creation divided flesh; marriage reunites it. Becoming one flesh could refer to sexual union although it's interesting that there's no mention of children here. Becoming "one flesh" could also mean one life shared in all its important dimensions. We might also see some oblique reference to gender equality as they are true partners and there's mutual recognition of some aspects of sameness between them. Maybe it points to a deep, mutual love between them. Or all of the above, which seems the best answer to me.

What I see in this account are the basic contours of marriage as God intended and intends. Catholic theology often establishes a contrast between what it was like "before the Fall" (of Adam and Eve) and after it when sin came into the world. In the beginning the relationship between the first two was good and, in fact, judged by God as very good. They were unashamed of each other and comfortable in their nakedness (their full personal presence) before each other. This changed after the Fall when such human acts as work and childbirth became associated with pain. The good times had passed.

In many forms of literature, there is often present this initial innocent state of existence before bad things happen. The account in the Bible is no different. Some commentators offer a psychological interpretation of this tendency to see some sort of original blessedness as perhaps stemming from some of our feelings about our own childhood, when things seemed better. Occasionally, we come across those who provide a social analysis of how things are and how things were and speak of those wonderful "good old days." I'm not interested in trying to argue for one interpretation or another. I'm only noticing how we sometimes claim that what was is better than what is. It seems to be a common human tendency.[9]

But I want to add an important theological point on this theory of past and present. Christians do well when they affirm that Christ came to restore God's original intent for creation. The overwhelming power of sin, strong as it is, has been overcome by the Christ event. We are saved from thinking that sin or sinfulness has won the battle. In our times, we live in the shadow of the Cross and the Resurrection of Christ. Despite evidence to the contrary, the intent of God for creation has, in the end, triumphed. And we should courageously live in that belief. Christ's victory can have a decisive effect on how we live. Do we live in hope or despair? Do we live in fear or in love? Hope and love are not theoretical concepts. They are the realities which underlie our every breath. We are tested by the powers of evil, but we need not be defeated. Goodness is not only possible, it's expected. And those who predict the eventual demise of the sacred institution of marriage will be disappointed. While marriage is going through some difficult times, it will survive. It is part of the hope that is the substance of our faith.

Love as gift

Christian marriage enriches each spouse because the love at its heart is fundamentally altruistic. Each person in marriage offers himself or

---

[9] An instructive account of how this kind of thinking works can be found in Stephanie Coontz, *The Way We Never Were: American Families and the Nostalgia Trap* (New York: Basic Books, 1992).

herself to the other in a somewhat paradoxical move that exemplifies the New Testament notion that it is in giving that we receive and in dying that we gain life. When we give of ourselves, we don't lose anything. But another truly gains. It's like what's called synergy where one plus one equals three. The result is more than the sum of the parts. The process of love, however, cannot be reduced to math or science. At its deepest level, it is partly mystery. It has aspects that are truly beyond words. On the other hand, hardly any other human expression has been more talked about, sung about, and written about.

How different genuine love is from a secular idea that one has to get all that one can, whether it be power or status or money or whatever, to be a success. Our culture almost equates the possession of a big house and car along with a large stock portfolio with success and happiness. In contrast, the Beatitudes praise poverty of spirit, meekness and forgiveness. To some of the modern world, these characteristics might appear more like signs of weakness and being a loser. I do not want to be judgmental of our culture here, but we all have to seriously ask where in today's world do we find genuine gospel values and where not. And I would add that this kind of inquiry relates directly to contemporary marriage because success there is directly connected with the quality and depth of the love in the marital relationship. Success in marriage is more about giving than getting.

Let's turn our attention now to gaining a fuller understanding of love. Some readers might be familiar with the three words in Greek that touch on the meaning of love. They are helpful in our breaking open for reflection the complex reality of love. First, there's "eros," which contains elements of desire, passion, sexual and interpersonal attraction, and the pleasure that derives from these. Taken alone, eros is often self-centered and is based more on personal need than a sense of giving. Nevertheless, eros can energize, excite, and create movement in a relationship.

The erotic side of life is sometimes criticized by religion as being evil and self-centered. And at times it can be that. But it can also serve as a positive force bringing people together. It can be a powerful source of enthusiasm for life and for connecting with others. I like to think of eros as an energy that awakens in us an appreciation of ourselves and others, a quest for beauty and a desire to be closer to others. It's like the first step in creating a deep relationship of love. Often our popular notions of romantic love are filled with eros. We fall into it. We're taken off our feet by it. It gives a bounce to our step and lights a fire within us. But it's only one aspect of love.

The second word the Greeks used for love is "philia." It's usually translated as friendship or "brotherly love" as we see in the meaning of the city of Philadelphia, the City of Brotherly Love. Friendship is a very important and often overlooked side of the Christian life. Jesus expressed his closeness to his disciples by calling them his friends. He saw that his friendship with them directly connected them to God. A religious community like the Quakers places friendship at the center of their understanding of Christian community. Sometimes "philia" describes family connections. Friendship can be thought of as having strong spiritual significance. Some canonized saints were known as having deep friendships like those of St. Francis of Assisi and St. Claire or St. Benedict and St. Scholastica.

We might reflect on how friendship is part of today's world. Do we commonly enjoy strong friendships? Do they have lasting power? Our culture today is strongly influenced by the ethos of the business and corporate world. We speak of others as colleagues, connections, and contacts. Friendship can be viewed as dangerous in the dog-eat-dog world of competitive business. People on the move often don't have the time to develop rich friendships. Social commentators note that so many of our interpersonal relationships are functional, meaning that they only exist to help a part of our lives. We use each other. We fit into each other's lives. We incorporate acquaintances into larger agendas and purposes. I mentioned above my valuing the exchange of peace during the Mass. I was once in a parish when at this special time during the liturgy, a gentleman next to me, after offering me a cheery greeting, passed me his business card. He sold insurance and my guess was that he had just attended a workshop on effective marketing and learned that he should take advantage of every social situation to gain potential clients. So I was offered the Lord's peace along with his company's insurance. I probably should have been bothered by his style, but at the time it seemed more laughable than totally out of place. We live in interesting times.

What's quite important to note here is that those who write about contemporary marriage often list friendship between the husband and wife as one of its essential and important components.[10] First, be friends, they say, and you will be able to deal with some of the inevitable chal-

---

[10] The qualities of good friendship are often mentioned in the research and publications authored by John Gottman (with Nan Silver), *The Seven Principles of Making Marriage Work* (New York: Three Rivers Press, 1999).

lenges of marriage. Marital love needs a rich experience of companion-ship, "philia," at its foundation.

Another word for love in Greek is "agape." This is the word used in St. John's First Epistle as a name for God.[11] Some theologians like to say this is God's proper name.[12] Agape is love turned into altruism. That means attention is directed to the one loved. It's sometimes called selfless love, but that can be deceiving because the self is quite actively involved in agapaic love. Other aspects of this kind of love go under the name of sacrifice, self-gift, unconditionality, and charity. Agapaic love is love written large. It is that kind of love that enables us to give ourselves, our attention, our time, our energy, our thoughts, our entire being to another as a gift. And we don't ask for anything in return.

In calling for this type of love, the New Testament invites us to love like God loves. God's love includes God's presence and power in our lives. God did not have to create us, but out of pure generosity, God did. To add to this, God's love is merciful and forgiving. Like the father in Jesus' story about the Prodigal Son, the Father runs out to greet and embrace us no matter what.

I see pure agapaic love as a standard or ideal that's out there before us and toward which we can direct our own love of others. Whether any of us can love exactly in this way is hard to know. Human motivation is complex and can be deceptive. To claim that we do this or that solely for the sake of another deserves careful consideration. We like to think we can love with no condition or limits and maybe there are moments when we do. But please understand that just because agapaic love is difficult and challenging does not imply that it is unrealistic. As with so many things in life, it's not our arrival that is crucial but rather our journey toward our goal. Movement in the right direction is what's important. Here, the image of life as a journey or pilgrimage is decisive. It's said that the importance of a pilgrimage is not as much the arrival at the sacred destination, but what the pilgrim experienced on the way there.

In all marriages there are times when we must act in love without the need for return. We will have to give up something we might enjoy so that the need of another may be met. These kinds of moments strengthen marriage. They show the depths of love. They take us beyond the simple give-and-take and beyond the demands of justice. In a sense, when we

---

[11] 1 John 4:8, 16.

[12] Michael Himes, *Doing the Truth in Love* (Mahwah, NJ: Paulist Press, 1995) see especially 7–21.

love with the abandon implied in agapaic love, we may feel a bit crazy. We certainly go beyond the expectations of our legal systems and ordinary calculations of what's to be expected in a relationship.

Early in my career as a theologian, I was giving a presentation to married couples on the nature of marital love. I mentioned agapaic love and connected it with the love Jesus had in dying on the cross for us. After my talk, a wise therapist asked to have a word with me. He cautioned me about connecting love in marriage with the love of Jesus. He was concerned about how some people might interpret my words as a blessing on a person's being a victim of another's destructive actions. He mentioned that over the years he had sought to serve those who had been abused. He shared with me that some of these people said nothing in their own defense for a long time because they thought that their suffering was something God wanted of them. Stephan Post is a moral philosopher and theologian who has written much about the nature of agapaic love. But he notes that such love is not to be thought of as total or radical self-denial or self-immolation.[13] Remember that Jesus and the whole Judaic-Christian tradition of moral reasoning speak of loving neighbor as oneself. Balance is important and we have a distinct responsibility to care for ourselves. We do not have to become a victim of another's destructive actions.

Whenever our descriptive language of love enters the realm of the beyond, we can be sure that we've entered the realm of genuine spirituality. Deep Christian love incorporates this kind of love when compassion arises for another. Caring for a needy parent, a child, or spouse often contains a rich load of altruism. We all know examples of this. Of course, we need not limit ourselves to those instances that are specifically Christian. The spirit of deep altruism exists in our world although it doesn't receive much public attention. However, it has recently captured the interest of social scientists because we all recognize its importance in all areas of life.[14]

What comes from this survey of ideas about love is that this orientation is far from being soft or ephemeral. Rather it touches the ground and has the power to transform every moment of our lives. Vatican II emphasized the comprehensive character of marital love. As you read

[13] Stephan G. Post, *More Lasting Unions: Christianity, the Family and Society* (Grand Rapids/Cambridge: Wm. B. Eerdmans Publishing Company, 2000).

[14] See Stephen G. Post, *Unlimited Love: Altruism, Compassion, and Service* (Philadelphia and London: Templeton Foundation Press, 2003).

the following quote, note how its descriptive language touches on many of the aspects of love that I have just described.

> Married love is eminently human love because it is an affection between two persons rooted in the will and embraces the good of the whole person; it can enrich the sentiments of the spirit and their physical expression with a unique dignity and ennoble them as the special features and manifestations of the friendship proper to marriage. The Lord, wishing to bestow special gifts of grace and divine love on married love, has restored, perfected, and elevated it. A love like that, bringing together the human and the divine, leads the partners to a free and mutual self-giving, experienced in tenderness and action, and permeating their entire lives, this love is actually developed and increased by its generous exercise.[15]

While couched in church talk, this passage includes some new affirmations about marriage that were not part of earlier church teachings. Note the emphasis on the human character of marital love and its application to the total lives of those married. Marriage is portrayed as human and holy, human and divine, human and spiritual. Married saints need not be portrayed as praying all day long or with eyes gently gazing into the heavens. Rather their attention is on their spouses; it is down-to-earth. Their spirituality is incarnational and relational, which we will describe in more detail in a later chapter. Their love for each other is expressed through sanctified sexuality. The experience of their love is connected with God's love, not in a competitive way but in one lifelong cooperative venture where marital closeness is a gateway, a symbol, and a genuinely human way of experiencing divine intimacy on earth.

---

[15] Vatican II, *The Pastoral Constitution on the Church in the Modern World*, 49.

Chapter Three

Can sex be holy?

Catholic theology and the life built on it are sometimes distinguished by a healthy use of the simple word *and*. We speak of Jesus as being divine *and* human. We use a similar formula to describe the church. We think of ourselves as being both sinful *and* graced. We understand our virtuous action as being a blend of God's grace *and* our human involvement. When it comes to describing Christian marriage, we now say that its purpose is both to deepen the love between the spouses *and* for the procreation of new life. That purpose directly applies to the sexual expression of love in marriage. Catholics welcome the greater breadth of meaning that comes from embracing the richness of life in all its dimensions.

The *and* dimension of Christianity alerts us to its central focus on relationships. God's own life is relational, first flowing from God's essential nature as Trinitarian and, second, because of God's intent to create a relational bond with Creation. Further, God's relational life is essentially one of deep love, the deepest imaginable. Over against any image of God as uncaring, distant, vindictive, or in any way negative towards creation and humankind is the Christian response that God is and always will be in a profoundly positive relationship with us. While our own daily lives provide us with many temptations to question or even reject God as loving, the fact remains: God is fully loving.

Within creation itself we can draw out signs or indicators of this relational aspect of creation. Following the fundamental insight of Albert Einstein, we see that all reality is, simply stated, relational. There are no realities in creation that are essentially solitary or independent. We can imagine such an existence. We can actually live and make decisions as if independence were possible. But try as we might, we cannot obliterate or deny our connection with everything that is. Absolutely everything!

In this chapter we attend to one of the most important relational aspects of our being. Genesis puts it this way: "So God created humankind in his image, in the image of God he created them; male and female he created them."[1] And as the passage later notes, God looked at all that he had created and said that it was *very* good.

Therefore, our sexual identity and all activity stemming from who we are as woman or man should be acknowledged, respected, and incorporated into our lives. While this is true for everyone, it is especially important for those married. So we now attend to that topic.

As we discuss sexuality and marriage we will first treat sexuality as an expression of deep love. In a later chapter that addresses children and marriage, we will fill out the description of marital sexuality by describing its generative aspect. Here we direct our attention to its loving aspect.

We begin with the affirmation that marriage in all its aspects is a celebration of love. A good Catholic wedding will usually include moments of exuberant festivity. Music, dance, food, and drink will be present at the feast just as the married couple request the presence of family and friends. For a wedding is not just the dry recitation of exchanged promises; it is also the joining of two persons of flesh and blood, the beginning of a journey which hopefully will include abundant moments of celebration and gratitude. It will also involve moments of silence and even anger, but we all hope the positives will greatly outweigh the negatives. Most of us who work in the field of marriage enrichment know a formula that was developed by John Gottman, a researcher on marriage who notes it's a five-to-one ratio that keeps marriage alive. Five positives for each negative. And I would suspect that if it's a big negative, it may take even more positives to keep the marriage alive.[2]

Most of the world's cultures have created festive rituals for weddings. And while wedding celebrations can get a little out of hand by costing a king's ransom for their enactment, most of the effort to make it happy and memorable is well worth it. After all, the hope is that we do this just once. And as I recall a thought from a college philosophy class, excess is a sign of a true celebration.

---

[1] Gen 1:27.

[2] See Evelyn Eaton Whitehead and James D. Whitehead, *Wisdom of the Body: Making Sense of Our Sexuality* (New York: The Crossroad Publishing Company, 2001).

No less a person than Jesus himself seemed quite at home at a wedding feast in his time. In fact, at Cana, he used the occasion to kick off his public ministry and his explicit effort in inaugurating God's kingdom on earth. That's what the Gospel of John offers us. Cana was not far from where Jesus grew up and whether the new husband and wife were friends or relatives, we don't know. John positions this event right at the beginning of his Gospel. It's like the opening line of a symphony establishing a tone and spirit for what is to follow.

Most know the story. As the wedding feast unfolded, apparently those in charge had not secured enough liquid refreshments for the crowd. Some have imaginatively suggested that Jesus came with his friends, hearty fishermen most of them, and there were so many that the wine supply was all but consumed well before the party was over. Mary, the mother of Jesus who noticed a potential embarrassment in the wings, nudged Jesus to do something. Jesus ordered that six water jars be filled. Those who were there remembered even this detail. Then was served some of the best vintage ever created. Those who understand this Gospel like to point out that much more was going on than simply making sure the wedding guests had enough wine. This was the "first sign" of what the Gospel terms "God's glory." And God's glory is that creation be more than we might think it to be. The water became something more. So did all of humanity with the coming of Jesus. And, given our present interest, so did marriage and everything associated with it. It was all part of the New Creation.

Again, think about the wedding feast. There was a moment when it was apparent that it was going to fail. Think of the possible humiliation of the couple and their family when guests were informed that the feast would end sooner than expected. In small towns people remember these things. Resources had run out. The party's over. Time to go home. But then Jesus steps in to create a huge sign, a dramatic gesture of concern and power that altered what would have been surely expected. Common water turns into delicious wine. The party not only keeps going; it gets better. New enthusiasm enters the feast because that's the way God wanted it to be.

In so many ways, the Cana event dramatized what's at the heart of all creation and what certainly is intended for every marriage: that it be a celebration of life and love. The possibility of chaos and death is overcome by God's supporting life and joy. John's Gospel in a way rewrites the original creation story in Genesis. In the beginning God breathed over the waters and created order from chaos. Here at Cana Jesus again takes water and transforms it as symbolic of life. Later in that Gospel it will be named as abundant life, life with the living God. We also know that Jesus will eventually take wine at another meal, the Last Supper, and transform it into his own blood which will become the foundation for the New Covenant between God and all God's people. Like I said, there's a lot more than meets the eye at this wedding feast. Jesus saved this day for those in attendance. This feast will serve to shed light on all the days that were to follow.

I often wondered what the couple thought years later as they re-called their wedding. No doubt, they were grateful and pleased that they had invited Jesus to celebrate with them. It was a great start to their marital journey. While it could have been a day of hardship, it resulted in being a day signaling God's New Creation.

Sex as expressing deep love

The Catholic Church over the last few years has experienced difficult times with its teachings and mandates concerning marriage and sexuality.[3] Part of this is due to the church's tendency to approach sexual matters from a careful and, therefore, conservative viewpoint. Looking at the long history of sexual morality in the church, the ideas and directives are often presented as being against certain behaviors. There's been little discussion of the church's positive views about the goodness and value of God's gift of sexuality.

Also, I have noticed that there often seems to be a bit of a bias un-favorable to the Catholic Church in the public arena. I can recall the national news reporting on the publication on Pope John Paul's major exhortation on marriage and family life in 1981. This particular publica-tion was the most detailed church document ever written concerning this important aspect of life. It was carefully crafted to provide pastoral support and encouragement to all Catholics. The publication was based on an international meeting of Catholic bishops at the Vatican in 1980. I had a strong interest in this document because I was a theological advisor to the American bishops at that meeting.

---

[3] For a well-researched, excellent, and easily read account of the history of the church in dealing with issues related to human sexuality, see Thomas C. Fox, *Sexuality and Catholicism* (New York: George Braziller, 1995).

But, in some ways, I suspect that most church views on this topic are almost doomed from the start because of preexisting assumptions about them. For instance, I still vividly recall the first news report I heard upon the release of the Pope's response to the meeting. The commentator simply stated that once again the Catholic Church has come out against birth control. End of report. What a scintillating first impression. Who would want to know anything else if it was just "more of the same?" The game is over almost right after it begins. It's not surprising to me that few Catholics have even heard of this publication. And it's also not surprising that many Catholics don't even have a basic knowledge of the richness of the church's teachings, especially in the area of sexuality, marriage, and family life if reports can be no deeper than "the church is against birth control."

My intent in this chapter is the claim that Catholicism offers an approach to sexuality in marriage that is intellectually challenging, deeply humanizing, and enriching. For instance, in the document just mentioned, the Pope, in addressing the meaning of sexual expression in marriage, wrote that it's not just a biological event, "but concerns the innermost being of the human person as such. It is realized in a truly human way only if it is an integral part of the love by which a man and a woman commit themselves totally to one another until death."[4]

This is high praise of the place of sexuality in marriage. It is not negative nor is it a notion that is restraining. One of the most important aspects of the church's view is that it affirms the great importance of marital sexuality. Sex in marriage, or in any other setting, is not trivial or inconsequential as our culture sometimes seems to imply. Sex in marriage is about deep and abiding love, about expressing and strengthening love between the spouses. Sexuality, like every other part of life, includes moral dimensions, just as everything important does. We recognize that God's gifts to us, which our sexuality is, always come wrapped with responsibilities. Yet when sexual activity is an authentic part of the love between the spouses, it is blessed, sanctifying, and a wonderfully important part of God's intent for creation.

This positive and respectful judgment about our being created sexual beings is not a new teaching. It's based on the long Judeo-Christian tradition of affirming the goodness of God's creation both in its totality and in each and every part. Some are surprised to learn that there's an entire book in the Bible filled with delightful praise of God's gift of sexuality.

---

[4] John Paul II, *Familiaris Consortio* (On the Family), 11.

It's called The Song of Songs. Some Bibles list it as The Canticle of Canticles or The Song of Solomon. This biblical book enjoys a long, colorful history of interpretation, most likely because it contains a series of rather sensual love poems.

Some readers have wondered whether literature of that nature should be in the Bible. They tend to interpret it as referring to something other than human love. They favor reading the book as an allegory of God's love for humankind. For them it is like a code, meaning that the reader shouldn't focus on what is actually said but the secret message behind it. That approach was popular for more than a millennium of Christian history. But current commentators conclude that it is what it is, meaning first of all, a description of human love celebrated between a man and woman. The collection of love poems might, in fact, be the words of songs sung during the lengthy marriage feasts that were common in ancient Jewish life.[5] We might also think of it as an elaboration on the Genesis passage describing all of God's creative work as good, even very good.

Its content rather graphically describes what happens when love ignites the relationship between a vibrant young man and woman. It portrays the physical beauty of both, as well as the pleasure they experience in their loving. If someone unfamiliar with this book happens upon it, they might think that someone playfully slipped in an extra book that really didn't match all the rest. I believe it is one of the Bible's most important parts. I would encourage everyone to read it. You don't hear its message at Sunday Mass. You can give your own interpretation as to why.

Here is a brief sampling of its treasures. Right at the beginning, it offers these words from the woman about the man she loves.

> Let him kiss me with kisses of his mouth!
> For your love is better than wine,
> Your anointing oils are fragrant,
> Your name is perfume poured out;
> Therefore the maidens love you.
> Draw me after you, let us make haste.
> The king has brought me into his chambers.[6]

---

[5] See Lawrence Boadt, *Reading the Old Testament* (Mahwah, NJ: Paulist Press, 1984).

[6] Cant 1:2-4.

A little further on, she provides us with more details of her interests.

> Upon my bed at night I sought him
> Whom my soul loves;
> I sought him, but found him not;
> I called him, but he gave no answer.
> 'I will rise now and go about the city,
> In the streets and in the squares:
> I will seek him whom my soul loves.'[7]

These are the words of a woman living in a strong patriarchal society. Notice her speaking the language of the heart and soul. Her desire for her beloved is evident. It is both personal and sensual. The general format of this biblical book is dialogical. Some of the love poems come from the woman and others from the man. Here is a sampling of the man's thoughts.

> How beautiful you are, my love,
> How very beautiful!
> Your eyes are doves behind your veil.
> Your hair is like a flock of goats,
> Moving down the slopes of Gilead.
> Your teeth are like a flock of shorn ewes
> That have come up from the washing, all of which bear twins,
> And not one among them is bereaved.
> Your lips are like a crimson thread,
> And your mouth is lovely.
> Your cheeks are like halves of a pomegranate behind your veil.
> Your neck is like the tower of David, built in courses,
> On it hang a thousand bucklers,
> All of them shields of warriors.
> Your two breasts are like two fawns,
> Twins of a gazelle that feed among the lilies.
> Until the day breathes and the shadows flee,
> I will hasten to the mountain of myrrh
> And the hill of incense.
> You are altogether beautiful, my love;
> There is no flaw in you.[8]

---

[7] Cant 3:1-2.
[8] Cant 4:1-7.

The language is earthy and fresh, arising from the culture of ancient Israel. It is sensual and sexual; it is not tarnished by any sense of embarrassment or shame. The fertility of the land, the flock and humans are all connected. A sense of celebration of God's good creation and the life it contains permeates the sensitivity shown in the vivid imagery of these love poems.

As already noted, many Christian commentators, particularly in the Middle Ages, saw The Song of Songs as quite imaginatively describing God's love for us. They were right, but not in the way they imagined. Today we would note God's presence in marital sexual love. In affirming a presence of God in human sexual life, we touch on the powerful idea of sacramentality.

God is there beneath the surface. In and through marital love and its expressions, especially those that are sexual, there is God. This is no small assertion. For most of its history, Christianity mostly tolerated as "necessary evil" human sexuality even in marriage. Its goodness was mostly associated with its procreative side. There were times when the pursuit of sexual activity in marriage simply for the sake of pleasure and comfort was considered sinful. Its primary (and only) purpose was to create new life. Its goodness and value for the relational life of the married couple was not emphasized at all.

While scholars suggest that these passages in The Song of Songs were wedding songs, it is also interesting to note that they were also used at funerals. A sense of God's continuing love had to be voiced especially in times of sorrow and sadness. The book of Job ends with the biblical claim that love is stronger than death. Maybe that same message is here in the celebration of love at the center of that moment when marriage, the harbinger of new life, is present. We can see this in a central assertion in the book that occurs toward the end. It stands equal to all the great words about human love ever written.

> Set me as a seal upon your heart,
> As a seal upon your arm;
> For love is strong as death,
> Passion fierce as the grave.
> Its flashes are flashes of fire, a raging flame.
> Many waters cannot quench love,
> Neither can floods drown it.[9]

---

[9] Cant 8:6-7.

Such a deep description of love is rare—even in the Bible. The most powerful forces known at that time, fire and water, are less powerful than the power of love. We are reading poetry so there is fluidity to the language. Nevertheless, what's suggested is the inherent power of love. Recall, too, that this is religious literature. That means it's an attempt to universalize about the nature of things, in this case, human sexual love.

I find it most important that such a positive and powerful description of sexuality is found in the inspired literature of the Bible. Created beauty and passion deserve their place in the writings that are received as God's word. I once came across a rabbinic commentary on the Bible that stated that God will hold us accountable for every pleasure given that we fail to enjoy. The spirit of this affirmation is here in The Song of Songs. For the married here is a reminder of the source of marital pleasure and beauty. Its author is the God of love. Sexuality is created by God and embedded in Creation as a gift to us. Like all God's gifts, it's set in the context of freedom and responsibility. Beauty is, as philosophers have noted, a mix of what's true and what's good. It reflects God's own beauty and love. It brings us to wonder and ask if all that's created is so beautiful, what must its Creator be like. Experiencing marital sexual love can become a path to understanding the deepest nature of God.

Traditional theology is quite adept at describing God's qualities as being reasonable and powerful, but what about the beauty of God? What about the beauty of creation? What about the fulfillments of ourselves through loving sexual experience in marriage? What insights about God might we gain from reflection on this particular aspect of our experience? In my office I have a wall hanging which reads: "Peace is seeing a beautiful sunset—and knowing who to thank." Let us add to that: "Experiencing deep sexual love in marriage is a wondrous gift—be sure to thank the one who created this."

Another question might be related to *all* the created beauty in the world. I have been impressed that often the great monasteries of the world sit in places of remarkable beauty. Was this not to give the monks moments of contemplation in which they observed what great earthly beauty surrounded them? The beauty of creation around them was like a launching pad for them to gain an immediate sense of God's presence. I am drawn to the poetic vision of the great Jesuit poet, Gerard Manley Hopkins, who saw the "grandeur of God" in the world around him. So many artists and poets have seen this dimension of God's creation, its beauty and magnificence. So too, I would assume, do married Christians.

The sacred and the sexual are drawn together in this book. The goodness of sexuality is affirmed. While parts of the Bible point to negative aspects of sexual activity, for instance, the behavior of David toward Bathsheba or the way the Canaanites used sexual relations in their fertility rites, here the purpose seems to be a simple affirmation of its goodness. Jesus will condemn a lustful look at someone other than one's own wife or husband but it's interesting to note how little is reported in the Gospels about sexuality. I would assume that Jesus accepted what his religion taught about it, with much of that teaching drawn from The Song of Songs. It is worthwhile noting his level of comfort as an unmarried man with those of both genders. Many commentators point to his familiarity with women although, for the record, I doubt he was married. With marriage being a quite important part of identity then and now, it would have been mentioned if he had been married. We have not a single word from him decrying sexuality in any way. And when he proclaimed the importance of love, I would assume that the life of the married would be on his mind.

God's word in Scripture is like a two-edged sword. It cuts deep. Its content is ever old and new—when heard with an open heart, it can be enriching and enticing, challenging and comforting. It can also drive us to reflect about both the meaning of our lives and the decisions we make in accord with our beliefs and values. In this part of our conversation, I want to affirm with clarity and vigor the basic goodness of our being created man and woman, man or woman.

Body joined with spirit

If I had to name one single philosophical influence that did great damage to Christianity, I would be inclined to name neo-Platonic dualism as the enemy. Its basic description of humankind was that it was composed of two separate realities, body and soul. While there are a thousand subtleties and interpretations of this dualism, I can only recount the feelings I had growing up in Catholic schools where we were told that we had these two parts: the body which mostly received a negative assessment and the soul which was like God. The body would eventually wither and die while the soul would exist forever. My spiritual life was mostly a matter of the state of my soul before God who knew everything I thought or said or did. Body and soul were presented as combatants in a war whose outcome determined my personal salvation.

If the soul won, I went to heaven. If the body won, it was to that other place I was sent and my stay was forever. On that foundation was built a list of don'ts, any one of which was a ticket downstairs.

Many of them had to do with "impurity" or the sexual side of my life. To fill out this picture, I remember that each of these sides of my identity had an advocate: an angel on my right side encouraging virtue and the devil on my left tempting me to sin. They were there all the time, especially at night when I walked through my neighborhood or when trying to sleep in my bed. The drama could be quite intense at times. One of the most helpful saving features of this whole ordeal was that if I slipped to the left, I could go to confession and reorient my path to what I was told was right. Ironically, I don't recall all this as particularly oppressive although I need to add that upon graduation from high school, I entered the seminary and religious life for a few years. Maybe deep down, I thought that environment would be a little safer for me than life in the world.

As I learned more about the history of philosophy and theology, especially through contemporary personalistic thinkers, I gradually brought body and soul together into an integrated appreciation and understanding of what it means to be a human person. I saw how my soul and body were different yet inseparable ways of being human. And both were good. Like everyone, I was a spirited body and a corporeal spirit. When I related to another in body, the spirit or soul was also involved. More spiritual moments had bodily effects.

The most influential thinker in the first thousand years of the church was St. Augustine. His own struggle to be human and eventually Christian was largely fought on a battlefield like that I just described. For many years he lived with a woman of a lower class and together they had a child. His mother, St. Monica, did not approve of this arrangement and eventually convinced Augustine to leave her and become a Christian. From his writings we see him as an intense, brilliant, and somewhat of a tormented person over the role of sexuality in his own life and in his relationships with women. In the end, he became a bishop of the church, a gifted theologian, and he founded a community of men with whom he lived. Maybe he found that a safer place.

At one time in his life, he was a follower of a group called the Manicheans. They deplored sexuality and were opposed to its use in procreation. Eventually he broke from them and wrote about "the goods of marriage" in part to convince others of what he viewed as their errors. He named these goods of marriage as sexual fidelity, children, and what he called the *sacramentum* by which he meant the permanent or sacred bond joining the couple together.[10] It's as if he marked the playing field, and most of the discussion for hundreds of years was focused around sexual ethics as they related to premarital and extramarital sex, the connection between sexuality and procreation, and the many issues surrounding marriage and divorce. Perhaps it's still that way.

Little was said in ecclesial circles until recent times about the holiness of marriage especially looking at it from its sexual side. In the documents of the Catholic Church one can still find exalted praise of consecrated virginity as a higher state of life. I will not take issue with that except that it's often set alongside marriage for comparison. Can we not affirm potential holiness and goodness in both states of life? Each can be sacred callings or vocations with each possessing its own sanctifying value.

Some of these older distinctions about good and bad, better or worse, came from the way body and soul were given separate and unequal rank in the general order of creation. The more we became "soul" or "spiritual," the closer we were to God. The more we were bodily in our actions, the further we drifted from God. Now many theologians see this as contradictory to the principle of incarnation which is rooted in the belief that God's Son became human, fully human, in the person of Jesus. All creation has been taken into the paschal mystery of the transformation wrought by the life, death, and resurrection of Jesus. Nature is graced; creation is sanctified. Humans are redeemed and blessed in the totality of their being. How well this is captured in one of the ancient creedal tenets: we believe in the resurrection of the body. It's time to say farewell to the dualism that weakened and emaciated the Christian appreciation of the bodily life. Deploring the life of the human body was never a good idea.

Nor was the idea that body and soul are separate, which is a current "heresy" in the secular world. As I see it, we do not live in a society that places too much importance on sexual life. In fact, society pays too little attention in the sense that it reduces the meaning of sexuality to recreation, selling cars and beer, and as simply a proof of popularity in a world of unsure and insecure people. People may think of their sexual lives as only for the moment or for the resolution of today's personal issue.

---

[10] See an excellent presentation of the history of the church's view of sexuality in Lisa Sowell Cahill, *Sex, Gender and Christian Ethics* (Cambridge: Cambridge University Press, 1996).

In contrast, the Christian view of sexuality is that it's deeply important as it directly participates in the indelible forming of one's personhood. Its power touches all of us, the married and unmarried. It's never
"just physical" because it operates in that pervasive connection between
the corporeal and spiritual aspects of our being. Like other aspects of
creation, it can open us to God's presence and communication. Being
created in the image of God, it can even offer us insight into God's nature
as passionately loving and life-giving. The respected Jesuit scientist and
theologian Teilhard de Chardin invited us to honor and respect creation
especially in the form of our humanity because "the Lord came to put
on, save and consecrate *holy matter*."[11]

While our sexuality plays an important role in human life, it is not
the whole of it. While some moderns want to see sex everywhere, thus
falling into a form of pansexualism, that's not how it is. Those versed in
the theory and practice of human development note that sex (as well as
other pursuits) can take over one's life, becoming an addiction or an
obsession. I recall my first acquaintance with this phenomenon in the
insightful writings of Rollo May where he pointed to the "daimonic"
tendencies of human nature when one particular aspect of life seems to
take over.[12] Those addicted to pornography may fall into this overemphasis of the sexual.

Sexuality is of central importance in marriage as a primary way of
not only expressing marital love, but also as a way of demonstrating
generous openness to new life. This pervasive acceptance and underlying
valuing of sexuality can almost be called a trademark in Roman Catholic
thinking. As Vatican II stated: "Married love is uniquely expressed and
perfected by the exercise of the acts proper to marriage. Hence the acts
in marriage by which the intimate and chaste union of the spouses takes
place are noble and honorable; the truly human performance of these
acts fosters the self-giving they signify and enriches the spouses in joy
and gratitude."[13]

In Christian marriage, the corporeal word of full sexual expression
is joined with the spirit of deep, faithful, and abiding love. This is an
honest word, a powerful word spoken with the whole body. Further, it's
important to keep in mind that all human language is both rooted in a

---

[11] Teilhard de Chardin, *The Divine Milieu*, new translation (Brighton, Portland: Sussex Academic Press, 2004) 65.

[12] Rollo May, *Love and Will* (New York: W. W. Norton, 1969) 123.

[13] Vatican II, The Pastoral Constitution on the Church in the Modern World, 49.

tradition and is formulated in unique ways especially as the word becomes more and more personal. Each of us has a certain style of communication. We have favorite words and phrases that are our own.

Throughout this book I have been emphasizing that each marriage will take on elements of uniqueness that arise from the unique personalities of each spouse. Each marriage is a kind of "new creation." We can extend this way of thinking to the way sexuality informs each marriage. Expressing ourselves sexually ought to be filled with authentic words and gestures that truly symbolize the interior disposition and personality of each person. Marital sexual love is not something one creates from a cookbook or applies to the marriage as if "one size fits all." Comparison with others is inappropriate. What's important is personal authenticity. Poetry asks how best to express deep love. How many are the ways we can do it. It is both a sign of our dignity and an expression of responsibility to communicate marital love in ways that best befit our lives. As the years pass by, we change. I recall a cartoon I saw years ago which showed an elderly married couple in bed. The husband was leaning over to his wife with a request, "Can I hold your hand?" She responds, "Not tonight dear. I have a headache." Ah, change.

We began this chapter with a thought about assumptions about the Christian and Catholic understanding of sexuality. We noted that undoubtedly there has been a bad press out there dismissing any positive and helpful role the church might have in informing its people about this important aspect of life especially for those married. I hope my "second opinion" given here helps correct this misconception.

Chapter Four

Why does marriage need rituals?

I t is five o'clock, the witching hour in our home. As my wife says, "The bar is open." She's not referring to a courtroom procedure, but rather to what some call "the happy hour." For us, it's usually a glass of wine. The transition between day and night begins at that time. Sometimes the smell of an oven-baked dinner fills the kitchen. Sometimes a pizza is taken from the freezer. And that's the way it is, almost every day.

Because there is a certain predictability and sameness to this event and others like it, we call it a ritual. Rituals draw from the almost limitless store of possibilities at any given moment, and craft a moment of special meaning. Repeated moments become rituals. Since rituals can diminish into routines of boring sameness, we often have to keep them fresh and alive. I want to focus in this chapter on marital rituals that spice our lives, give depth of meaning and purpose to special parts of our lives, and create memories that accumulate and form the substance of our allotted time on earth.

I especially want to underscore the importance of rituals directly connected with Christian marriage. Most will think almost exclusively of the rituals connected with the wedding, but I want to push the boundaries of important ritual experience in marriage to include other events like wedding anniversaries, the births and birthdays of family members, family reunions, and the like. I also want to include events like our evening ritual with a glass of wine and a slice of cheese. I want to embrace the daily texture of married life where the day is broken open by a moment of togetherness. To qualify for the pantheon of marital moments, the activity doesn't have to be exotic or even that special. In fact, the more ordinary the better because it can then be more frequent, and let's not forget the importance of affordability.

Survival during good times and not so good make a marriage. So one of the most important qualities in marriage and family life is that of resiliency. This is the quality of life directly related to the ability to survive difficult challenges. By now, you might have noticed that I have adopted "challenge" as a basic dimension of marriage in these times.

Marital life is experiencing trying times. Some welcome the present situation. They say that the freedom in which marriage now survives, freedom from family pressure, freedom from outside incursion, freedom from limitation especially for women, freedom to create a marriage that is unique and flows directly from the distinctiveness of each spouse is a welcome change for many.

Yet floating marriage on a sea of freedom is bound to include significant change from earlier times. Before the current era, marriage survived in the protective embrace of larger social structures, like the extended family and the local community. Its relational dynamics, its daily life, were observed and often determined from the outside. Today most marriages are just the couple, moving along a path that they themselves mostly decide. It's more a private matter just between the husband and wife. The survival of any given marriage will therefore depend almost entirely on the inner life of the marriage. This is a much more fragile social arrangement than before. Greater marital freedom has changed almost everything.

Some judge that this free-floating aspect of marriage has a dangerous side. It creates societal worry. Marriage has always been one of the primary foundation pieces of a healthy society. Some point to the high incidence of marital failure through divorce, which most now agree stands in the range of 50 percent for marriages beginning these days. They occasionally bemoan the later and sometimes delayed marriages which can mean children might come into the world in a home where its parents are not married.

In noting the higher incidence of marital breakdown, the blame is attributed to a variety of factors: among those mentioned is increased individualism, self-centered consumerism, lack of willingness to commit, poor messages from mass media and the like. They believe marriage could be strengthened by more effective marriage preparation, stronger restraints preventing marital separation, more effective therapy services to help the married when they face difficulties, and a general tightening of social sanctions relating to marriage. Some will be so bold as to call for a whole cultural restoration of the beliefs and values that support marriage more fully.[1]

And there's worthwhile truth in all these discussions. We need to talk about marriage much more than we now do. David Mace, a pioneer in the marriage enrichment movement, used to say that marital life can become the great secret that no one talks about. Marriage can become so private that it virtually disappears from the public arena.

Part of this concern comes from a conviction that strong marriages build better families and a healthier society. Churches will also be strengthened if the fundamental social bond of marriage is sound. All agree on one point: better preparation for marriage is needed. Some claim, with perhaps a tinge of cynicism, that some couples invest more time and energy in buying an automobile than in selecting a marriage partner.

How did the church get into the wedding business?

I'm not going to argue that church weddings should be abolished, but there is something to say about the overemphasis that is often given to the wedding. It's big business with some estimating the average wedding costs in excess of $20,000. Weddings keep florists, musicians, caterers, renters of formal wear and wedding apparel in business. I wrote my doctoral dissertation on the Theology of Marriage according to the great Swiss theologian, Karl Barth. He once commented that Catholics have a great theology of the wedding, but not much about the marriage thereafter. There was truth in his thought.

I once worked in a Catholic parish that had many weddings. I helped with preparing couples for their wedding liturgy and their marriage although their attention seemed mostly focused on flowers and the guest list. One couple came to our program with their newborn baby. Respectfully I asked them why they hadn't gotten married before they had their child. Their answer was immediate. They didn't have enough money for the wedding!

Of course, great attention to weddings has been around for a long time. Remember Cana! Also the beginning of something as wonderful and important as a marriage deserves special attention. Good rituals are

---

[1] See a comprehensive and convincing discussion of this in Don Browning, *Marriage and Modernization: How Globalization Threatens Marriage and What to Do about It* (Grand Rapids: Eerdmans, 2003).

important. They can capture in the combination of meaningful words, gestures, music, and other symbolism that which words cannot quite express. For example, the act of exchanging rings during the wedding can communicate much to imagination and memory. The ring symbolizes unending love.

And weddings in the presence of the assembled Christian community are all the more important. The couple stands before close family and friends as they publicly declare promises of immense significance. During their shared life of marriage up ahead they may need the assistance and support of the community. Certainly they need God's help because they are embarking on what surely will be a perilous journey filled with unknowns. In the Catholic Church marriage is a sacrament, an event denoting the sure presence of God and a promise of God's helping grace.

It's an interesting story to recall how marriage came to be thought of as sacred and as a sacrament during the first two thousand years of church life. Part of that history is how marriage came to be celebrated before a priest, or now a deacon, with a ritual in a church. What follows is a brief overview of that history which will lead us up to the current ritual through which the church celebrates what should be for the couple, a major turning point in their lives for the good. We start, as we must, with Jesus and quickly pass through roughly twenty centuries of church history.

Marriage was always considered to be good and holy, up to a point. But at times specific church attention to marriage was not apparent. Its value was overshadowed by the emphasis on virginity, celibacy, and the monastic life. For most of the first thousand years, the church simply went along with the marriage customs of each culture, which for the most part were drawn from the Greco-Roman world and later from the Germanic tribes. As was noted earlier in our study, marriage mostly involved families and clans with not a lot of attention given to the wishes of the couple.

While Jesus did not address marriage often, when he did, his words were strong. For instance, he noted that what God had joined together in marriage, human effort could not separate.[2] Involving the action of God in something humanly created is no small matter. This single line in Mark's Gospel exerted significant influence in the church's understanding of marriage throughout history.

[2] Mark 10:9.

Marriage was thought of as involving God's presence and participation. The general position of the Catholic Church in divorce was and remains that neither the church nor human society has the capability or the power to sever the bonds of Christian marriage. That means that not only will the church not separate the wife and husband from each other through divorce, but the Catholic Church *cannot* do this. What God has done is fixed. Only death will end the marital union. The church approaches the marital bond with full respect and absolute seriousness. And it is this understanding of Christian marriage that guides the church in dealing with marital breakdown. These words of Jesus play a foundational role in determining the Church's understanding of Christian marriage.

Jesus also stated that "whoever divorces his wife and marries another commits adultery against her; and if she divorces her husband and marries another, she commits adultery."[3] Jesus places marriage into the framework of lasting human relationships which involve not just the couple, but also the active work of God. Today's more secular approach to life will be challenged on this point because of the way we separate the human from the divine. Christian faith connects our seemingly ordinary lives with God. We are laced into God's dealings with our world whether we acknowledge this or not. God's presence, of course, is neither obvious nor apparent. The eyes of the faith-filled penetrate externals to disclose the spiritual depths of creation in all its manifestations. Jesus specifically called attention to God's involvement with marriage. Although it's present in a thousand other places, God's role in marriage was so important that Jesus chose to explicitly single it out so that we would not overlook it.

In another gospel report, Jesus reformulated the moral law around the issue of adultery.[4] Jesus noted that the sin of adultery not only involved the physical act, but also interior attitudes and thoughts. We also find a similar view in the Sermon on the Mount.[5] Jesus is making more concrete the Mosaic Law or the tenth commandment that prohibited coveting or desiring the neighbor's wife. Then Jesus added an important feature to this mandate by speaking of all this as a matter of the heart.

References to the heart were like a code signifying the center of the person. The heart was thought of as the very center of the person, the

---

[3] Mark 10:11-12.
[4] Matt 19:9.
[5] Matt 5:27-28.

source of what's deep inside us, the region of the soul, the core of each one's individuality. Attend to matters of the heart and you will have covered what's essential. Thoughts of the mind, movements of the will, and acts of love all find their origin in the heart.

By singling out lustful tendencies, Jesus wasn't so much pointing to human sexual excitement or passion, but rather to a self-centered desire to use another person for one's own satisfaction. Manipulation or use of another person can "objectify" the other, depriving that person of his or her own God-given sacredness. Further, we know that people can fall into the pit of sexual addiction where the sexual aspect of life becomes all-encompassing, diminishing freedom, and preventing other aspects of the self from developing. In the history of Catholic theology, this was described as concupiscence, which was viewed as a powerful bodily tendency that could overwhelm one's best and most sacred identity.[6]

Having established the view of Jesus that sexuality and marriage were important aspects of life in God's Kingdom, we really come across very little in the writings or practice of the church concerning marriage. St. Paul ran into a question as to whether people should get married, stay married, or remarry if widowed, given the belief that the world was soon to end with the second coming of Christ. His response was wise and practical by saying that he really had no specific information to share about this. If asked his own personal opinion, he said that he would discourage marriage at that time because of the assumed imminent end of this world. Put simply, he was wondering why get married if it will be only for such a brief time. But in the end he simply left it to the individual to make the best choice with these words. "I say this for your own benefit, not to put any restraint upon you, but to promote good order and unhindered devotion to the Lord."[7] So, using today's colloquial language, it would be like saying "why bother?"

During the next few centuries there were occasional opportunities to defend the goodness of marriage against those who questioned its value. Most followed the lead of St. Augustine (354–430) who wrote that marriage was good because it brought new life into the world, it helped people (especially men) deal with concupiscence, and it provided a symbol of Christ's love for the church following the words of the Epistle

---

[6] This topic is discussed at length in addresses given by Pope John Paul II. See his *Theology of the Body: Human Love in the Divine Plan* (Boston: Pauline Books and Media, 1997) 135–80.

[7] 1 Cor 7:35.

to the Ephesians. Occasionally teachings would connect marriage with the creation account in Genesis and note Jesus' presence at the wedding feast at Cana. (What's worth noting, however, is that the description of this event in the Gospel of John says little about what Jesus thought about marriage. His attention was focused more on those famous jugs of water.) Much more was written during these early centuries valuing virginity.

We have some local accounts of church blessings being given at the time of marriage, but they are always directed to the bride. The need for bridal purification is not without historical precedence in the Judaic-Christian world. I have found it most interesting that a so-called nuptial blessing was not given to the groom until the liturgical reforms of Vatican II when blessings for both the bride and the groom were created.

During the earlier centuries of church history there was a split between the eastern and western branches of Christianity, between Constantinople and Rome. The eastern approach was not touched as much by the anti-sexual philosophies of the west and thus had a more inclusive and wholesome approach to marriage. The Eastern church developed spiritual rites for marriage with the priest playing a more important role in the ritual. By the fifth century their wedding ceremony included a crowning of the bride. The priest also joined the hands of the couple as a symbol of their being one in Christ. Recall, too, that priests in the Eastern tradition were themselves allowed to marry, a tradition which remains even today.

In the west, except for Augustine's naming one of the "goods" of marriage to be sacrament (which for him meant simply a symbol of Christ's love for the church), marriage was not considered as part of the church's official sacraments until the eleventh century when Peter Lombard listed marriage as one of the seven special sacraments of the church. And it was not until the sixteenth century at the Council of Trent that it was *officially* incorporated and named as a sacrament. The full story of this late acknowledgment ought to mention that the Catholic Church did this only after some of the reformers like Martin Luther claimed that there were only two sacraments, Baptism and Eucharist, because they were the only two clearly instituted by Christ as reported in the New Testament.[8]

[8] Most of this historical material is drawn from Edward Schillebeeckx, *Marriage: Human Reality and Saving Mystery* (New York: Sheed and Ward, 1965) and Joseph Martos, *Doors to the Sacred: An Historical Introduction to the Sacraments of the Catholic Church* (Liguori, MO: Liguori Press, 2001).

As civil power became more unreliable in the late Middle Ages, the church began to take over more of the responsibility of maintaining societal order. We have already discussed how for much of its history marriage was organized and supported by the concerns of families and the wider community. After all, much of the wealth of people was tied to the land and other possessions, and ownership was often affected by new marital arrangements. So the church entered the world of marriage, at least in the beginning, with as much interest tied to its worldly as well as its spiritual meaning.

By the eleventh century the presence of a priest was required at church weddings throughout Europe. Two hundred years later the church became concerned about clandestine or secret marriages mostly because of the practice of women being forced into wedded life. This signals a very important change in church policy because it clearly shows a concern for the quality of Christian marriage. The importance of free consent given at the time of the wedding gained center stage at that time.

Let's pause here to reflect on that change. Spiritual consciousness both in the individual and in society has a history. What's implied in what I'm describing, namely the gradual realization of the importance of marriage for the persons involved, did not happen overnight. And while I'm highlighting the ritual and legal dimensions of marriage, it's important to note that these changes did not happen only in the halls of church governance, but more importantly they were happening in marriage itself.

During the Middle Ages, a new form of literature and thought came on the scene. It's generally called courtly love, and most historians claim that we find evidence for this new spirit of relationships mostly in the context of court life. From it come images of brave knights defending the honor of princesses and other women of the court. Wandering troubadours composed music praising the work of Cupid and ways of love that seemed to arise and disappear with abandon. Something was happening in the land, a new awareness of what could happen between a man and a woman that would spark excitement, deeds of valor, and even the offering of one's life for the sake of the beloved. Historians like to note that this "courtly love" was mostly limited to the upper echelons of society, but that's because, I would add, that's where we have the records. What I wonder is this. Might a new appreciation of love between wife and husband also have been a part of this movement? Might a gradual revolution have been taking place in marriage itself moving it from a mostly biological and secular union to one that is more personal and spiritual? Cultural changes of this nature may take centuries to unfold in their fuller dimensions. So we need not be forced to think that we now live in a blessed time of awareness and meaning and consign past generations to being in the dark. Some instances of deep love in marriage might have been around for a very long time. I would certainly hope so.

Sometimes the church and its theologians "get into the act" when there are what's viewed as false teachings in the wind. On the edges of the church one often finds those who adopt sometimes bizarre beliefs about life. Often they adopt a strong dualistic view separating body from soul or some other separation. They align themselves with what they judge as good and condemn others. One of these groups was called the Albigensians who condemned bodily existence because they thought that the body imprisoned the soul and that this world was ruled by the devil. They numbered many followers in France and Italy beginning in the twelfth century. While St. Paul wrote that we are to glorify God in our bodies, these folks thought ill of the body, especially when it came to matters sexual. It's worth noting that individuals and groups despising the bodily dimension of human life seem to make regular appearances throughout Christian history. Fortunately the church uses its inherited wisdom and common sense to ward them off.[9]

In this case the charge was led by St. Dominic who founded a new community of preachers and theologians called the Dominicans. One of its first members was one of the greatest of all Catholic theologians, St. Thomas Aquinas. Like others, he called attention to the consent given by both partners entering marriage. He wrote about how this promise played an active role throughout the rest of the marriage. Aquinas studied the whole library of existing secular and sacred writings. He was drawn to the down-to-earth philosophy of Aristotle which focused on the natural world. Of course, Aquinas viewed the world as created by God and filled with God's presence and continued support. He also taught about the essential goodness of humanity and drew ideas from earlier philosophers, both Greek and Roman. He was especially influenced by the Roman philosopher and rhetorician, Cicero, and his treatise on friendship. Aquinas integrated the notion of friendship into his comments on

[9] For more about them, see Michael Woodward, "Albigensians," in Richard Mcbrien, ed., *HarperCollins Encyclopedia of Catholicism* (San Francisco: Harper, 1995) 28–29.

Christian marriage. For him, marriage was a community of nature transformed by God's grace, making marriage a sanctified state.[10]

In reality, not much was added to the theology of Christian marriage until the twentieth century with the work of Vatican II. The already mentioned Council of Trent in 1563 underlined the importance of sacramental grace given to the married couple through their exchanged vows and afterward as need arose. What's most known about this church council was that it "circled the wagons" of the Catholic Church in response to the efforts of both church reformers and certain humanists who were not supportive of the authority of the church, especially as it was judged to impinge on the secular order. Trent decreed that the marriage ritual follow a specific form, namely that it be performed publicly by a priest and before two witnesses.[11] As we can see, there was an evolving concern within the church over marriage. Some might see this as a power move, but I would rather interpret it as a growing concern for marriage as an important part of the Christian life.

Marriage is a matter of public concern. Common sense leads us to conclude that while a couple may consider their marriage as "only their business," nevertheless, because of how society is constructed, marriage is one of the important building blocks of society, and, I would add, even more seriously, of the life of the church. We are interconnected with each other in countless ways. One of the less fortuitous aspects of the philosophy of romantic love is that it separates lovers from all else. It places them in a kind of psychic bubble that constitutes their whole imagined world. Belief in this understanding of love and interpersonal life, which contains large doses of irrationality, fantasy, erratic and erotic feelings, has led to many broken hearts and broken lives. I don't want to turn marriage into something that looks like a business contract, but there are many aspects of married life that are pretty prosaic and down-to-earth. Marriage is for the whole of life, a quality that not only refers to its temporal existence, but even more to its day-to-day role in human survival. I would add that some parts of marriage—like who prepares the meals, who cleans the house, who takes out the garbage and, if children come, who takes care of dirty diapers—are part of the raw materials for constructing happy and holy lives within Christian marriage.

---

[10] Thomas Aquinas, *Summa Theologiae*, III, 65. See also Schillebeeckx, 325–43.
[11] Council of Trent, Session 24, *Tametsi Decree*.

You are invited to the wedding of . . .

Rituals can be like empty boxes whose value increases depending on what one places inside them. A handshake can embody the intent of two leaders of large nations to establish peace between them. It can consummate a major business transaction between two global corporations. It can symbolize a reunion between friends who have not seen each other for years. Or it can be a meaningless gesture, done perfunctorily, between two strangers who care little about each other. Same gesture, quite different meanings.

We already noted that weddings can be big business. They can become one long and expensive photo op and not much more. They can also be a transformative moment for the bride and groom, a deeply spiritual crossroads, a profound time of deep love and commitment. The opportunity is there.

We've already noted that at least in Western history, marriage moved from being an event of the family to an event involving the couple, their families and friends, and the church. In general, marriage has always been valued, with its religious and spiritual value increasing through the centuries.

In modern times, great attention was given to what might be called the moment of the sacrament, which was the exchange of vows during the wedding ritual. In the Roman Catholic Church the proper ministers of the sacrament of matrimony are the couple themselves with the priest serving only as a witness to their actions. Today many theologians look at the wedding as an essential beginning of the marriage with its sacramental dimension extending into the full future of the couple together. This is a major advance in the theology of Christian marriage and we will devote a full chapter to the meaning of marital sacramentality later.[12]

But ritual expressions, especially those operating in the realm of the sacred, often require a time of preparation, a period of getting ready so that one is fully open and available to "the big moment" and to all those moments following. After all, we hope it will last a lifetime. For that reason the Catholic Church has created a variety of educational and formational opportunities for those entering the sacred state of marriage. Following the thought of Pope John Paul II, this period of preparation involves virtually all of one's early life, which is thought of as remote preparation for marriage.[13]

---

[12] See Chapter Eight.
[13] Pope John Paul II, *Familiaris Consortio* (On the Family), Section 66.

The ritual of Christian marriage is a moment of grace, a time when God is present and active in the life of those marrying. With their vows being an expression of deep love, it is exactly there that God is, because God is love! That's the essence of God according to the New Testament, especially as described in the Gospel and letters of John, the beloved disciple.[14]

In a sense, God's love permeates the love between the two spouses in the wedding ritual when the couple invites it. While God is always present in creation, and especially where there is love, God's presence is even more compelling at certain times in life. The Catholic Church celebrates and acknowledges these times through the enactment of the seven sacraments of the church. While Christian marriage was the last sacrament to achieve this status, the Catholic Church has come to respect and point to the moment of exchanged vows as one of those very special moments.

Ideally the couple fully enters into the ritual, allowing its power to touch their minds and hearts. Given the details and complexities of some weddings, this is not always an easy accomplishment. Worry about the details, about family guests, almost anything can get in the way of focused attention on what's really important.

From the standpoint of the church, the beginning of Christian marriage also signifies an addition to the total church through the creation of a new "domestic church." Drawn from the history of the early church, this designation powerfully expresses this aspect of the church begun with the wedding. Pope John Paul II says that Christian marriage is a special enactment of God's love in relational form. He wrote that ". . . the central word of Revelation, 'God loves his people' is . . . proclaimed through the living and concrete word whereby a man and woman express their conjugal love."[15]

The wife and husband are truly ministers and instruments of God's love for each other. Begun at the wedding, this pattern creates a flow of God's life and love between them that extends into the total future of their life together. In marriage, grace is personalized. One of the challenges of the married is to be aware of or notice this happening. One of the reasons the church took so long to affirm the sacramental meaning of marriage is because marriage is also part of the natural order. It existed

---

[14] For a theologically brief but brilliant account of this, see Michael Himes, *The Mystery of Faith: An Introduction to Catholicism* (Cincinnati: St. Anthony Messenger Press, 2004) 5–18.

[15] Pope John Paul II, *Familiaris Consortio* (On the Family), Section 12.

before the coming of Christ and it exists everywhere. It's not obvious that it is also a church event, a holy setting, a sacred context for God's basic dealings with us.

The heart of the wedding ritual is the public expression of the marriage vows or promises. They are expressed in the presence of God as well as the assembled community. They are, in a sense, audacious and courageous words because the substance of these promises extends into the unknown future. We never know what's around the corner and some people are almost paralyzed when thinking about this. Marriage requires the virtue of hope or trust in God.

One of the more important changes in the church's description of Christian marriage happened in the documents of Vatican II when the language of legal contract found in Canon Law and other church documents was replaced by words of personal covenant. Covenant is a richer concept involving both God and humanity. It attends to the personal uniqueness of those entering this new relationship. It clearly implies that one is entering into the territory of the sacred.[16] Contracts tend to be more impersonal by focusing on the exchange of goods and services. Covenants are more encompassing as they extend to the full range of sharing life with another. While this embraces the full expression of love through sexual intercourse, it also includes the full sharing of life's joys and sorrows as well as all those actions needed to maintain life together. Pope John Paul II speaks of the total gift of self that is part of the bodily exchange that's part of marriage. He saw in the creation of man and woman, "a nuptial meaning" given to the body by God which expresses the full sharing of self that marriage ideally becomes from its beginning at the wedding until the death of one of the spouses.[17]

A final area worth mentioning focuses our attention on what traditionally has been called the faith readiness of the couple to receive the sacrament of Christian marriage. Most Catholic pastors are quite aware of the situation where people come to the church requesting a church wedding (their language). While they are baptized, they often have not formally participated in the life of the local church for a long time. The same pope addressed this situation in his response to the questions of many bishops from around the world about this pastoral difficulty. He

[16] For more about this, see Julia Hanlon Rubio, *A Christian Theology of Marriage and Family* (New York: Paulist Press, 2003) 73–75.

[17] Pope John Paul II, The Theology of the Body: Human Love in the Divine Plan, 60–63.

recommended pastoral sensitivity and openness to their requests. I quote him at length to capture the nuances and full import of his thinking. Two passages illustrate the depth of his response.

> The sacrament of matrimony has this specific element that distinguishes it from all the other sacraments. It was a sacrament of something that was part of the very economy of creation; it is the very conjugal covenant instituted by the Creator 'in the beginning.' Therefore the decision of a man and woman to marry in accordance with this divine plan, that is to say, the decision to commit by their irrevocable conjugal consent their whole lives in indissoluble love and unconditional fidelity, really involves, even if not in a fully conscious way, an attitude of profound obedience to the will of God, an attitude which cannot exist without God's grace.

Following this affirmation of what might be called implicit faith, he goes on,

> Nevertheless, it must not be forgotten that these engaged couples by virtue of the baptism are already real sharers in Christ's marriage covenant with the church, and that, by their right intention, they have accepted God's plan regarding marriage and therefore, at least implicitly, consents to what the church intends to do when she celebrates marriage. Thus the fact that motives of a social nature also enter into the request is not enough to justify refusal on the part of pastors.[18]

Those who come to the church for marriage with dormant or weak faith provide a wonderful opportunity for the church to welcome the couple back to the church and re-evangelize them into the fuller life of God's people. These intentions can be an important part of the preparation offered by the church for receiving the sacrament of matrimony.

It is advised that at least these two general areas of learning be a part of such preparation. First, the couple can increase their knowledge about each other as persons. Oftentimes, our secular approach to marriage serves to limit real exposure due to a fear that full revelation might prevent the marriage from happening if one or the other really found out the truth. This is a most dangerous situation because of the gravity of the decision and its far-reaching consequences. One should want to know

[18] Pope John Paul II, *Familiaris Consortio* (On the Family), Section 68.

everything about the other: their deeper values, any major mistakes that were made in the past, and all about the other's thinking about crucial elements of marriage like sex, money, religious beliefs, and the like.

Excellent inventories are available and used in many preparation programs to help place on the table all significant areas that will affect the intended marriage. These instruments make explicit not only those areas where there is disagreement between the engaged parties, but also where they align in agreement. A decision is being made to bond with another person of immense complexity. Entering marriage requires full freedom and awareness not only about what's ahead in terms of challenges and possible difficulties along with an acquaintance with the skills needed to deal with them, but also full knowledge of all the intricacies of the other person.

Second, the couple has the right to know the full Christian and spiritual meaning of what they are intending. They need to know how their Christian faith, however weak it might be, connects with the new life they are entering. They do well to learn how the love of God and love of neighbor connect with each other. They may need an updating in understanding their faith as it pertains to adult life. They need to know the Catholic Church's position on various social issues. Finally they deserve to receive the best thinking of the church concerning sexual issues, especially as they pertain to responsible parenthood. Many come to the sacrament with only a dim memory of what they learned as a child in religious education classes. In other words, there's plenty of opportunity to be further catechized into the mysteries of Christian faith during marriage preparation.

When the Catholic Church began to list Christian marriage as one of its sacraments, it felt that it also had to show that Jesus instituted this sacrament. While there was no direct evidence of his having done this in the gospels, his presence at the wedding feast at Cana was given as support for marriage.

I think it's more worthwhile to use Cana as an example of having a good time around the celebration of the wedding. In general, I don't think we capture enough of the happiness and joy associated with being a Christian. Jesus was obviously a partygoer. St. Luke's Gospel has him attending ten separate feasts during his life. In fact, that Gospel reads like the social calendar of Jesus as he made his way from place to place.

Christian marriage is a celebration of God's love made tangible in the lives of a man and woman who have found each other, gotten to know each other, and fallen in love with each other. This is grounds for celebration. We don't feast on the fact of love enough. And weddings, with the associated rituals of the day, provide a wonderful opportunity to be with family and friends to create with the new couple a sacred and holy feast. We all know that sometimes these gatherings get out of hand, as we say. But we need to be reminded that gospel means "good news" and that we were created as loved by God to enjoy all that God gives us.

Of course, weddings are but a beginning. In some ways, the best follows. The development of love and life are discussed in the next chapter.

Chapter Five

What makes marriage last?

fter class one day, I was walking across the campus with one of my students. He said that he couldn't figure how anyone could do it. "Do what?" I casually asked. "Mortgages," he quickly replied. "Some of them can be as long as twenty or thirty years. I could never do that!" I smiled as I thought about a future lecture in my course that would discuss lifelong marriage. I wondered what he would think about that!

Years ago I learned a simple principle that can help us deal with such long-term realities. It's drawn from the life sciences. It goes like this: If there's no growth, there's decline. To survive, living beings need constant nourishment. All living things sit on the boundary between life and death, survival and extinction. To survive, we must keep it on the plus side.

So, you might ask, what does this have to do with marriage? A lot! Marriage, like everything else alive, needs constant attention if it is to endure. It responds to all the processes of growth and decline that apply to the rest of life. In answer to the question of why some marriages make it and some don't, an initial response could be this: Those that embodied relational growth from the wedding day on, survived; those that didn't, often died. So what today is called marriage enrichment is not an add-on, but a basic survival need for making it through the years ahead with sanity, joy, and happiness. And despite the frequency of celebrity divorces, there are many others who make it all the way to the end.

Marriage enrichment can be thought not as a burden, but as part of what everyone does to live a fuller, more enriching life. Marriage is always a perilous adventure based on what theologian Richard Gaillardetz calls "a daring promise."[1] While this may seem obvious, it's surprising that we don't hear much about the need for relational growth in marriage. Once the wedding is over and its expenses have been paid, the couple is more or less left alone as they settle into marital life. This notion of "settling in" can give the dangerous impression that the challenges of significant relational development are more or less over.

How does the church view all this? Does the church promote expectations of marital growth? Some may not think so, but I have discovered interesting evidence to the contrary. For instance, I was a little surprised to read in a papal letter about Christian marriage written more than seventy-five years ago words challenging the couple to grow in their relationship. The author of this letter was Pope Pius XI and he issued his teachings about marriage on the last day of the year, 1930.[2]

The one essential marital task

I think it helpful to start with the big picture, the overarching framework that every couple needs to create an enriching and joyful lifelong marriage. I'm not talking about doleful endurance, but a shared life of happiness that will have its hard times, but in the long run will provide both wife and husband with perhaps the best part of their whole life. Of course, successful achievement of this goal is far from simple. It takes day-by-day desire and effort. When long-term married couples are asked their secret, the phrase most commonly heard is that they "worked on their marriage" every day. A second common reason we often hear is that they both had a sense of humor.

Deceiving, and even dangerous, are those simplistic approaches we read about in glossy magazines where marital survival requires taking "five easy steps to marital bliss" or by putting "more spice in your marriage with a tropical vacation." Every marriage is a deeply complex matter, second only, I would add, to the intricacies of the parent-child relationship. It demands the best of our wisdom, the full strength of our energy. Most of all, it will demand many conversions of the heart, which, in a biblical sense, involve the very center of our being.

[1] Richard Gaillardetz, *A Daring Promise: A Spirituality of Christian Marriage* (New York: The Crossroad Publishing Company, 2002).
[2] Pope Pius XI, *Casti Connubii* (On Christian Marriage), Section 49.

This fundamental task involves both an interior change of attitude and many external actions that symbolize the interior change. Recall that I have noted that each marriage is unique which means that each marriage accomplishes this task in its own way.

So what is the task? Put simply, the task is to deepen genuine interpersonal love, day by day. There's no time off, no time out. The game of marriage, as we're now looking at it, begins with the wedding, and ends with death. Think about great athletes who are always seeking ways to improve themselves. To stay "on their game," they have to be working on it all the time. Similarly, as married persons, we're always in need of fine-tuning and expanding our marital lives in view of the conditions of the moment.

So in a very real sense, we are engaged in a lifelong process of "becoming more married." I realize that this way of presenting marriage is different from considering marriage as a state of life or as a fixed relationship determined by rules and sanctions. For me, and I would assume for most, marriage is a living reality, and as such is more of a verb than a noun, more of a dynamic set of actions than a fixed state of being.

From a structural point of view, this task places us on an odyssey from the narrow confines of the individual or private self to the broader world of self and other. This will almost always be a precarious journey, filled with fear and risk. Psychologists have come up with the phrase, "comfort zone." That's where we feel totally safe, unafraid, and unchallenged. The original comfort zone was when we were in our mother's womb before being born into the "hostile" environment outside. Marriage is a kind of hostile, if not demanding, environment, especially when it's deliberately and faithfully pursued.

Of course, after a very trying day, we may need to find our personal comfort zone to unwind, relax, and catch our breath. Most mental health professionals see stress as one of the great killers of our time. They recommend such ways as quiet meditation and relaxed breathing so that we can still the anxiousness within. We each need to be the best we can be for our married partner and most see value in taking time alone as part of this process. We assume that the overall goal remains not only to stay married, but grow toward an ever deeper relationship.

This primary task is built on a foundation that affirms the full equality between the wife and husband. I often return to this value because I consider it one of the great revolutionary social gains of our time. The value of gender equality invites us to look beyond roles or occupations and seek to balance the process of responding to each other's needs, interests, and desires. While recently giving a retreat to married couples, I came upon a very helpful image for describing the difficult and precarious nature of maintaining equality in marriage.

In my workshop I cut a small piece of wood in the shape of a triangle. To my symbolic wooden image, I added a Popsicle stick. Thus I created a visual of a playground apparatus we're all familiar with, the seesaw. I first ask those in attendance to recall a time when they were on a seesaw and when each person tried to remain suspended in total balance. Then I asked them to recall a time when as children, they were stuck at the top, held there by the power of the one at the bottom. The seesaw maintained a fixed position. No one could move as long as the person "in power" remained firmly planted on the ground.

The moment of seesaw balance could only be maintained by the constant cooperative action of both on the seesaw. If one side started to descend, that person had to "lighten up" by moving slightly toward the center of the board. In the world of science, the creation of this kind of balance is called homeostasis. In biology this process describes the ability of an organism to maintain internal equilibrium by adjusting physiological states. When a cell has too much sugar, it seeks starch. If too acidic, it tries to find a base chemical.

Marriage is a complex balancing of give and take. If one is always giving and the other always taking, the "system" is unbalanced. This is clearly an unhealthy situation from the standpoint of marital growth. In good marriages both partners look out for the other. They try to keep the score even. They're attuned to the need for justice.

This primary task of marriage unfolds through a series of steps, the first involving the transition from single life to being married. This can be all the more challenging for those who marry a little later in life. We all have the tendency to form habits over time. We get used to doing things our way! Living as a single person, one does not need to accommodate the presence or the needs of another person. For instance, we can be fully in charge of our personal living space. If we don't mind living in a messy place, if we're perfectly content to do dishes once a week or clean the bathroom each July (whether it needs it or not), so be it. We can watch all our favorite TV programs, enjoy our peculiar dietary habits, and go to bed and get up almost whenever we want. We can have our own friends, favorite pastimes and interests, and there's no one around to complain or prompt us to change anything. None of this is bad, but it all might become problematic when we move from single to married life.

I don't think this point needs much elaboration except to note that old habits may not be easily changed—or, if necessary, reversed! Here's another complication. It is sometimes said that when it comes time to marry, we choose a person with whom we enjoy many common interests and pursuits. But it's also noted that our intended may be someone who fills in areas where we are lacking. They may be accomplished in areas where we are not. I know of people who live quite disorganized lives. Their clothing is strewn everywhere. They seem to have no idea where they left last month's pile of unpaid bills. In fact, they really don't know exactly how much money is currently in their bank account. Who wastes time keeping records, they might say. They often forget to send "thank you" notes for gifts received. Or answer emails. They may occasionally miss a doctor's appointment. In a word, they dwell in a world that is rather disorganized.

This kind of scattered person meets a person who not only knows exactly his or her current bank balance, but also has a thoroughly organized sock drawer and bathroom! How interesting, notes the person with no clear awareness of how many socks he or she owns or where they might be located at this moment. Opposites attract! That is often true. We sense our personal deficiencies and are attracted to bonding with someone who has what we need. This may seem a practical and desirable strategy to pursue.

Yet there's a catch. Those interesting and temporarily attractive differences often become concrete stumbling blocks into the marriage. The shy person who marries an extrovert begins to complain that they have to go to so many parties with friends and business colleagues. The religious person who marries to help the other find God begins to complain that the spouse doesn't want to go to church each Sunday.

Welcome to the multifarious world of marriage. So the task of the married is to create a shared life where the needs of each person are respected and adjusted to. Again, it's no easy matter. Over time we become comfortable with our eccentricities, although they are not seen as that while we are living the single life.

Besides dealing with the peculiar habits we bring into our marriage, there is the deeper matter of the exigencies of living a deeply interpersonal life. This involves countless acts of attentiveness and listening. It may require a new kind of investing where what's called "social capital" is built into the marriage.[3] Most people are familiar with accumulating

---

[3] See Scott Stanley, *The Heart of Commitment: Cultivating Lifelong Devotion in Marriage* (Nashville: Thomas Nelson Publishers, 1998) 118–23.

capital assets. Well, translate that process into the world of marriage. Just like "every penny counts" in the financial world, so every positive and negative relational event flows into the lives of the married.

Further, the results are just as telling. While there's a side to marriage that defies simple calculation because, after all, it is primarily a matter of the heart, there's a side to it that can at least be imagined in finite terms. And there, a deep logic prevails. I once heard a therapist say that he begins counseling troubled couples by asking them to fill out a time chart for a week. Together they examine the filled-in ledger the next week. What they look for are times when there's at least a potential for experiencing positive couple moments. Often in marriages on the brink, there are either few or none.

Lifelong happy marriages are built one positive relational act at a time. Simple gestures of attention, kindness, and support strengthen the love relationship between the wife and husband. One additional note to this process might be helpful and that has to do with the very nature of love between persons, especially in marriage.

We all have special ways that we want to be loved. Some wives enjoy the gift of flowers especially as a surprise. Some husbands enjoy a well-prepared dinner. I don't want to fall into prescribed roles here because we can just as easily switch the example to say the wife would enjoy a well-prepared dinner by her husband, and the husband might really cherish the gift of flowers from his wife. The point is that we all have preferences on how to be loved. With that as a starting point, we tend to express love for another in ways we want to be loved. We don't inquire as to what the other would like, we presume it. Sometimes we're lucky and it works. But there are a million examples where it doesn't. The day after Christmas is a good time to see this in action as both men and women return Christmas presents given the day before by a loving spouse. You can guess the rest.

So part of the marital conversation should include some mention of the love needs of each partner. This may be one of the more prosaic dimensions of love, but it's still important. Again, this turns the relational dynamic toward the beloved other. The narrowness of the self is challenged. And while we all wish that our spouses knew us well enough to guess our needs, in this world at least, this rarely happens. It's another reason why clear and honest communication remains an essential in good marriages. While hopefully there will be moments when we brilliantly intuit exactly what our husband or wife "always wanted," most of the time it will boil down to a knowing based on the actual expressing of desires and needs. While this may seem to take some of the glamour away, in the long run it's always a plus to replace guesswork with actual research data.

All of the above contributes to building a lifelong marriage. It also contributes to a rich relational spirituality, a topic we will devote a whole chapter to later on. While love has its mystical and even mysterious side, it's also a very down-to-earth reality. It's founded on an interpersonal attraction that draws two people together, sometimes with a force equivalent to objects falling from the sky to the earth. Maybe that's why it's called "falling in love." At times, it may seem outside our control. Much is written about this dimension of love. It's the subject of countless novels and movies. And, I would add, it's God-given, a sort of built-in energy source that helps us set aside our shyness or interpersonal fears thus allowing us to connect or "make the first move." Sometimes called romantic love or eros, it remains one of the most powerful forces within us. And because it can be traced to God's creative act, it's very good.

But you don't need an advanced degree in psychology to know that this kind of love can be a bit like a giant firecracker in the night sky. It burns brightly for a while, but then diminishes. It's absolutely wonderful for starters, but for the long haul it will need to be replaced by other dimensions of love, the kind of love we have been discussing here. Too many marriages end in the first year or two. My guess is that the initial fire was extinguished by other realities which were unable to sustain the love that was once there. Sometimes good marriage preparation can decrease the likelihood of these short-term unions. Unfortunately, some prepare for marriage by concealing more than by revealing their true selves to each other. Their thinking is clouded by the fear of separation and the naive belief that once married, they will live happily ever after. Strong emotions can get in the way of clear thinking. Some call this the "halo effect" that supposedly protects the premarital relationship from the buffeting winds of challenge. We can all step outside this reality and clearly describe its shortcomings. Yet when under its power, clear thinking is about the last thing desired by the couple. They truly live in a dream world.

But let's not dwell on failure. Our purpose here is to support marital success. So we affirm the value of developing relational capital, ever-deepening marital love, and a set of practices that truly serve to strengthen the relationship. Let's explore further aspects of such development. We'll begin with a reflection on how the passage of time serves Christian marriage.

The blessing of time

In many ways we are captivated by the mystery of time. With major timepieces all calibrated to an atomic clock which keeps exact time, with our mobile phones and computers offering us digitized time every time we look, with many of us carrying various forms of planners directing and keeping an account of our every moment, well, we've come a long way from those days when time was measured mostly by sunrise and sundown. Now, every minute counts. This influences what is now our biggest complaint. Is it that we don't have enough money or we're pulled down by poor health? No, not at all. Put simply, most of us feel that we never have enough time. Our lives are over-scheduled and we stress out because we can't get everything done. It's gotten so bad that even children now carry schedule books!

How each of us deals with this situation will vary from person to person. Maybe we have to plan our time more carefully. Maybe we have to make an honest evaluation of various aspects of our lives and then decide what's most important. We can try to gain more leverage of what we do and what we skip. In today's world, most will admit that there never seems enough time for all that we want to do. We must make choices, meaning that while some wonderful activities will be selected for our precious days, some will be set aside. Maybe they will be done on the proverbial "rainy day." In the end, how we spend our allotted time is an indicator of what we believe is most important.

Here, I want to connect marital vitality with how we use our time. Know first that the last thing I want to do is escort us on a guilt trip. Over the years, I have found guilt to be among the least productive and energizing of all human emotions. It pushes us to the ground when we need to fly. It takes away our self-respect when we most need the energy that comes from within. So rather than begin by offering a long list of "shoulds" that will surely induce guilt, I would rather begin with a quiet reflection on the value of time and its place in the grand order of things.

As I read the creation accounts of the book of Genesis, one of the first things I notice is that God, the Creator, "took time" to create. Whether it was six twenty-four hour days or 13.7 billion years, I care not, at least for this reflection. And whether God created other universes which may have existed before or during our life here, that too, while a most challenging idea, is not my concern here. I simply want to underscore the amazing reality of God-given time and the fact that our existence is marked by how we exist as temporal beings.[4]

The great German philosopher, Martin Heidegger, was mystified by the idea that we are temporal creatures. What particularly caught his attention was the fact that our days are numbered. We will all die. Nevertheless, he noted that many people seem to live their lives virtually oblivious to this unassailable fact. He saw this as a genuine tragedy because he believed that a strong awareness of our impending death could awaken us to a much deeper experience of living! For him, death was not a morbid preoccupation, but rather the great energizing thought. Live as fully as you can because there is no guaranteed tomorrow.

The world is filled with stories of people with terminal illnesses who appear to live their final days, whether it be a day, a month, or even years, with incredible intensity. Are these people blind? Do they not realize that they are about to die? Of course they do, but that awareness is what gives them the push to become extremely responsible about how to use the limited time now given to them. They savor each moment. They treasure each day. Should not all of us do the same?[5]

In God's wisdom as revealed in the Christian tradition, we are given one lifetime here on earth. Upon our death, we hope to experience eternal life. But in reality, we have very little insight into what awaits us after we die. We trust it will include life with God and with all the others who have preceded us, especially those we have loved. But the boundary between this life and the next remains opaque, as God has intended it to be.

And much the same can be said about all of our tomorrows. We walk through our lives shadowed by the unknown and the mysterious. I like the phrasing of the English Jesuit, Gerard W. Hughes, who sees God as laying down before us one surprise after another. We are not in control of huge parts of our lives.[6] Some of it, yes, but not the whole. But we need not despair, because our lives are supported by the power of Someone who loves each of us very much. In such circumstances, why

---

[4] A delightful resource on this topic is Bonnie Thurston, *To Everything a Season: A Spirituality of Time* (New York: The Crossroad Publishing Company, 1999).

[5] Being a basketball junkie, I refer you to the biography of Jim Valvano, celebrated college coach. Written by his brother, it celebrates Jimmy V's time after he was diagnosed with the cancer that eventually took his life. Bob Valvano, *The Gifts of Jimmy V: A Coach's Legacy* (Chicago: Triumph Books, 2001).

[6] Gerard Hughes, *The God of Surprises* (London: Darton, Longman and Todd, 1985).

not follow the advice of Jesus, which I would summarize as an invitation to trust in God's care and enjoy the ride.

Of course, some very important aspects of our lives are under our control. The decisions we make create the texture for many of the major and minor features of our lives. God created us with the gift of free will and God fully hopes that we use this remarkable gift to the maximum.

In Daniel Boorstin's rich account of the history of discovery, he singles out the discovery of time as absolutely foundational for human life as we know it today. We forget that before an appreciation of historical process developed, humankind mostly believed that it was positioned in what Francis Bacon called "the cyclical monotony of nature." This amounted to feeling rather impotent because one was trapped in an endless cycle of repetition that repeated itself without significant change year after year. Life became an endurance of circular events, much like walking through a maze that had no end, no exit, no opening to a life of greater freedom and fulfillment. One was literally stuck in the place and the condition into which one was born.[7]

One of the implications of our new worldview is that we can and should be as creative as possible. Every day offers us an option. Freedom is there from God for the taking. So use it! Color your life with its many possibilities. As Nadine Stair said in her later years, "If I had my life to live over, I would start barefoot earlier in the spring and stay that way later in the fall. I would go to more dances. I would ride more merry-go-rounds. I would pick more daisies."[8]

Exercising genuine creativity and inventing newness are extremely important for life in general, and marriage in particular. Freedom is now a major factor helping us to succeed not just in marriage, but in about everything else too. We have mentioned that Christian marriage has been traditionally described as a "state of life." Once married, one was positioned, some would cynically add "incarcerated," in that state for the rest of one's life. While this approach had its merits, it failed to address the need for growth and development within marriage. It lacked an understanding of the important historical or temporal aspect of human life. Thus the wedding was thought of as a destination, not as the beginning of a long adventuresome journey.

---

[7] Daniel J. Boorstin, *The Discoverers: A History of Man's Search to Know His World and Himself* (New York: Random House, 1983).

[8] Taken from a set of wonderful poems edited by Sandra Haldman Martz, *If I had my life to live over* (Watsonville, CA: Papier-Mache Press, 1992) 1.

Like all other things sacred and human, each marriage has its own story or history. And we are truly cocreators with God of that history. And significant change will happen after the wedding, for better or worse. Repressed dimensions of our personalities may surface. We age over the years which always bring changes. The law of gravity comes into play as parts of our bodies lean more to the earth's center. But we need not only focus on what some consider negatives.

Communication can improve, intersubjective sensitivity can increase, and inevitable marital hurts can yield to reconciliation and a deepening of marital love. For centuries, major aspects of our understanding of human life were flat and lifeless. Humankind, in general, might have become too accepting of the status quo and impotent in the face of challenges. This was most unfortunate. Now we have grown in our appreciation of human power to make things better. Married couples can seek help from trained professionals when they face difficulties. Experts in the complexities of interpersonal life can assist all of us to make our way through the sometimes rough waters of marital life. Where in the past there might be despair, now there is more room for hope.

Here I am reminded of one of the greatest historical events of recent history, the bloodless revolution that occurred in South Africa as that society set aside the apartheid system of racial inequality and created a system of government and life that affirmed the equality of all. I believe that something similar occurred in the social revolution that affirms the full equality in the marriages of women and men. Looking at the total history of marriage, this is indeed a major change that truly challenges us to be married in a new way. In that sense, I see history as an advance for humankind at a very fundamental level of life.

Achieving that equality with love is an ongoing challenge. It will only be achieved in marriage through thoughts and actions day by day, year by year. Christian marriage thus possesses a dynamic aspect that invites its participants to embrace the challenge of a fully shared life, including time with and for each other, not once, but thousands of times.[9]

When couples embrace this challenge with open hearts, they push their humanity into ever deeper realms of vitality. They deepen their spiritual lives and contribute to the wondrous venture that builds "the body of Christ" on earth as it is in heaven. To love another in marriage

---

[9] A quite perceptive presentation of this kind of thinking is found in Maggie Jackson, *What's Happening to Home: Balancing Work, Life and Refuge in the Information Age* (Notre Dame, IN: Sorin Books, 2002).

is to give to him or her the gift of your time. Allowing another this place of prominence is no small matter. We share our personal lifetime present to the needs of another person and we do this spontaneously and freely. That's why marital love is so important. It opens one to another. It invites the other to enter the deepest part of one's life. This is the greatest of all gifts. The gift of oneself. It is what Jesus said at the Last Supper and is repeated at each Eucharist: "This is my body which is given up for you." This is the primary model for Christian living, the giving of the self for another. In Christian marriage, this happens in ways that are both wonderful and sacred. Even when it boils down to who takes out the garbage today.

The time after the wedding offers a series of opportunities which invite expressions of marital love. This time can extend the days of the wedding for fifty years or more. The time can be wasted, but it can also become filled with God's presence and grace in action.

We live during a time when freedom is both affirmed and valued. But the value of freedom is like an empty container until it is filled with meaningful gestures of the human spirit. Each marriage will survive when the partners in it freely decide that the best use of time is in serving love, which is like the fire in the hearth. It needs a continuous supply of fuel or it will die.

Difficulties along the way

I have searched the literature. I have consulted with therapists. I have asked family members and friends. When teaching or when presenting retreats to married couples, I have asked whether anyone has ever known of a married couple who has negotiated the rough waters of marriage without a single difficulty. Is there such a reality as a totally happy marriage where there was not a single event of conflict, a bad day, or a disagreement between the wife and husband? That is the question. I'll bet that I've asked it in one way or another of thousands of people. But at least until now I have not found a single positive response, not a single untouched marriage. So I am ready to make right here a quasi-scientific conclusion: Every marriage on this planet experiences at least a few difficulties, a time or two when some friction is felt in the sacred space between the spouses.

So I would have to conclude that the goal is not to avoid all conflict or disagreement, but to find ways of surviving these storms. And that is no small challenge. Some say it's not *what* you fight about but *how*.

The ideal is clearly to move through times of discord and disagreement in ways that both feel heard and respected. And when final agreement or reconciliation is reached, both freely and as willingly as possible accept what's decided.[10]

A deeper question is the greater *why* question about marriage. Why should marriages last a lifetime? What is so wonderful about staying together until there is a parting at death? We will discuss in more detail Christian marriage as sacrament in our final chapter. But here, I would mention that lifelong marriage is symbolic of God's lifelong connection with us. The good news of the gospel, no, the great news of the gospel is that God's love for us is steadfast and enduring. We pull away from God, and God follows us. We may attempt to break with God, but God is there with divine adhesive to reconnect us. God is persistent and resolute. God desires our closeness and "works" tirelessly to ensure it.

To make this relationship a reality in our world, God has joined the relational events here, so to speak, with the reality that comes from heaven. Love of God and love of neighbor are basically the same reality, the same commandment from God's point of view. Jesus knew this, lived it fully every day he walked on the earth, and gave this way of living to his disciples. Today the church affirms the reality of love in its many dimensions and manifestations.

These words are being written early in the pontificate of Pope Benedict XVI. In his first encyclical letter to the church, he chose to focus upon the very reality that is at the heart of Christian marriage. He writes the following: "Marriage based on exclusive and definitive love becomes the icon of the relationship between God and his people and vice versa. God's way of loving becomes the measure of human love."[11]

Sometimes differences between husband and wife will remain and, as it's said, we'll just have to agree to disagree. Feelings can be terribly hurt and at times one or another or both may have to "give in." As should be apparent by now, I firmly believe that every marriage has its difficulties, some, more than others. But I would hope that through the whole of their life together, both the positive and negative sides of this, their love for each other would remain intact. It may be bruised or shaken, but it's still there.

---

[10] See an excellent presentation on dealing with specific problems in John M. Gottman, *The Seven Principles for Making Marriage Work* (New York: Crown Publishing Inc., 1999) 157–216.

[11] Pope Benedict XVI, *Deus Caritas Est* (God is love), 11.

Much has been written and said about the role of conflict in marriage, besides its inevitability. Of primary importance is that the differences between wives and husbands be acknowledged and put on the
table. Marriage should be a safe place for airing differences, resolving
conflicts and, if anger arises as it often will, admitting to that as well.[12]
This enduring aspect of marital love has been singled out by those who
research lasting marriages as a critical reason how couples can, in fact,
engage in conflict, but still remain married. They can confront each other
without fearing that any particular conflict will tear them apart. Their
love is stronger than the need for agreement or for always having to
"win" every marital debate. In other words, it's love for the other, as
other, for the well-being of one's marriage partner.

Conflict avoidance, however, has been known to enter a marriage
or two. Sometimes family background plays a role in this. Some families
spend most of their time "walking on eggs" so as to steer clear of discord
or arguments. It's as if each family member lives in a glass cage. Family
secrets are hidden in a locked vault. Such evasion, however, costs the
family dearly because it pushes family members apart. They end up
feeling more alone than connected.

Then there's the situation where there is a big unresolved issue
between the spouses and they do all they can to avoid even thinking
about its presence. Here in Montana, where I now live, we call it "the
grizzly bear in the living room" syndrome. Outsiders would notice its
presence right away, but those who live there ask, "What grizzly bear?"
and answer, "We don't see one."

Most experts in marriage and family life will say that dealing openly
with differences can create interpersonal growth and intimacy. Wrestling
with conflict can be a way of both testing and strengthening real love.
But it can also be a way of entering some very difficult, although very
real, aspects of life, especially married life. We don't always get our way,
and in a good marriage, we will surely experience many moments of
great sacrifice, frustration, and outright disappointment. We like to imagine marriages where there is total harmony, where each one's desires are
fully met by the generosity of one's spouse, but we need to turn on the
lights. It doesn't happen.

---

[12] An excellent discussion of this can be found in Judith S. Wallerstein and Sandra
Blakeslee, *The Good Marriage: How and Why Love Lasts* (Boston: Houghton Mifflin
Company, 1995) 143–49.

The French say "viva le difference" to accentuate and celebrate the differences between the sexes, but there's also another way of reading this God-created reality. Sometimes our human nature seems to prefer, like Narcissus, a mirror image of itself in another. In creating marriage, God has guaranteed that this will not happen. There are significant differences between all humans, and these are accentuated by the differences between man and woman. What's challenging is to see this as a blessing, as a wonderful aspect of God's incredible creative imagination and wisdom.

I like to imagine life as a floating trip down a long, winding, and sometimes perilous river. The Middle Fork of the Flathead River runs a few miles from where I live. It offers exciting white-water rapids, challenging narrows, and places where the floating is easy. It's just as we experience life, especially marriage. On this river there are places where it's good to enter. A favorite place is about ten miles north of West Glacier, the western entrance to majestic Glacier National Park. It's helpful to have a reliable and sturdy raft and a good guide who knows the river and its personality. A daylong ride on this scenic river leaves one with memories for a lifetime.

The challenge is much the same for lifelong marriage. It too will have its rocky moments. It will have to pass through perilous narrows. And it will have those times when one can simply lie back and enjoy the passing cliffs and mountains. And the best part of all is to say that one has run the full course.

Chapter Six

How do children fit into marriage?

The contents of this chapter are not intended to be a guide for how to be a good parent. A quick search on the Internet will reveal that there are hundreds of fine books already dealing with this topic. Here I want to sketch a theological or spiritual approach to the topic. Much less is written about this aspect of parenting.

There are two areas worth considering from this standpoint. The first involves the decision to have children, "to be open to life," as this is sometimes described in church teachings. The second area will include reflections on the ministry of parenting. In describing this role of parents, the late Pope John Paul II wrote the following. "The sacrament of marriage gives to the educational role (of parents) the dignity and vocation of being really and truly a 'minister' of the church at the service of the building up of her members."[1] He then referred to the thought of the great Catholic theologian, St. Thomas Aquinas, who did not hesitate in his writings to liken the role of parents to that of the ordained priest.

We begin with a general comment on God as the source of all life. All gifts that are given to us by God come with a card that reads, "Share this with others." Divine gifts are not to be treated as personal possessions or private property. They are not to be locked in a vault or frozen in a plastic container. They are to be used, and a basic rule is that they be used for others.

God's greatest gift to each of us is the gift of our life. I am here writing these words, and wherever you are, you are reading them. Both of us would do well to give thanks to God for this moment. If God withdrew

[1] Pope John Paul II, *Familiaris Consortio* (On the Family), 38.

from us for a second, we would return to our original condition before creation. We would become nothing!

All humans are invited by God's Spirit to share our lives and ourselves with others. This responsibility knows no exceptions. We have learned from the sciences that in creation all life is interconnected. At its beginning and all the while it continues, life requires the right conditions of a hospitable environment. Human life, in particular, needs not only healthy surroundings to survive, but a desire to continue living.

With our existence comes the wonderful gift of freedom. That means we have to want to live. We have the capability of being quite creative in keeping ourselves alive. Think of Tom Hanks in the wonderful movie, *Castaway*, where he was able to use the meager resources he found on a deserted Pacific island, along with an ice skate, a soccer ball, and a few other items, to stay alive.

Married couples do well to see themselves as "receivers and givers of life." This includes creating new life in begetting children. For as long as we can remember, marriage was intimately tied to this purpose. From its earliest beginnings, people desired the continuation of their kind, however arduous its accomplishment may have been.

Today, we face this challenge with a more refined understanding of those acts needed to generate new life. The decision "to have or not have children" is now much more under the control of the couple. Aware of our advances in our understanding of biological processes, the church calls married couples to act responsibly in this important aspect of marriage. "Responsible parenthood" is part of Catholic moral teaching. Later we will address more fully how the Catholic Church views the exercise of this responsibility. Here, however, I want to focus on the deeper issue of having a sense of being gifted with life with the intent of sharing this gift with others. In Christian marriage this touches on the decision to become parents.

All are familiar with the fact that marriage now not only possesses a personal side, but also has become a matter of sometimes heated political debate. For instance, the question is now asked who should be allowed to be married and who should be considered as married in the eyes of society and its governing bodies. I have already stated that I agree with those who hold that Christian marriage involves the union of a man and a woman. Yet I also remain quite concerned that the civil rights of all permanent partners be respected. I believe that we must be careful not to discriminate against anyone based on sexual orientation or any other human quality that makes each of us who we are. This "marriage debate" shows no sign of lessening. It's a very complex issue and contains, as I've noted, both personal and political ramifications.

Today, much the same can be said about the connection made between marriage and parenting. It's both personal and political. It wasn't always so, but it has come to be that way in our time. For instance, it is not uncommon to learn that single persons are becoming parents either through biological methods or by adopting. Further, through death or divorce the number of single or lone parents is growing every year. In other words, the traditional connection between marriage and parenting is no longer as conventional and common as it once was. And while these new trends are well worth serious examination and discussion in both church and societal circles, I will focus here on a specific connection between married life and parenting. This focus, however, is not without its own questions in our times of huge social change.

Looking at the overall picture of marriage today, we see that perhaps for the first time in history we encounter among many couples a clear separation and even a deep ambivalence about any essential relationship between marriage and having children. To be married is one decision and to attempt to have children is another. Many married couples decide to wait a while until they think about having a child. There are many reasons for doing this. Sometimes they feel a need to be more settled economically or in their careers before they add another responsibility to their lives. Sometimes they want to finish their education. Sometimes they just aren't sure. When I married years ago, this division hardly existed. In fact, my wife and I purchased a book on parenting on our honeymoon!

Research today indicates that more married couples than ever simply don't want children. Their reasons vary. Some seek a lifestyle that would be easier to attain without the burden of having to raise a child. We live in a society where both wife and husband often have full-time careers. Some seriously worry about bringing any more children into a very troubled world. Some have medical fears associated with high likelihoods of possible birth defects. And some may want children, but can't because of biological reasons.

One thing is for sure. The arrival of children in a marriage surely changes everything! To overlook this fact is to fail in understanding the many responsibilities connected with raising children. The government reports that it will cost an average of $200,000 to raise a child from birth to eighteen years of age. When factoring in the time required for parenting, the energy expended, the loss of sleep and sometimes, as parents report, their sanity, well, it's understandable why some couples simply pass on the parenting option. That's one side of the debate. Now let's look at the other.

The decision to parent

One of the most important virtues needed by all of us in times of uncertainty and rapid change is that of hope. It's especially needed when a married couple is making that important decision about having a child. When you become a parent, you create a new world for yourself with a population growth of at least one. And the new situation is so permanent. Of course, we need not take a dim view of this. There are a thousand positive aspects of being a parent, although, to be honest, our culture often seems more aware of the negatives, at least if we use news reports as our primary source of information.

In reality, parenting is a rich blend of positives and negatives. Ask any parent. The pendulum can shift in a second. One minute the parent is enjoying with great delight little Addison playing with her cereal, but when she decides to fling her gooey food at her baby brother, well, let's just say the climate rapidly changes.

And the challenges continue. Most parents with little ones often hear the horror stories associated with rambunctious and recalcitrant teens. "Wait and see," they are told. The bright happy days with little ones will soon become the dark and dismal days of adolescence. Some of this is true, but like all generalizations, there are a million exceptions.

We also know of situations where children, once thought to have left home to establish their own financially independent existence, call home announcing their return, with all their stuff, at age thirty. What's common about all parent stories is that once children come, your life changes!

Let's return to our discussion about hope. Hope is a virtue and attitude that looks ahead into the unknown and concludes that God's help and our human effort will be adequate to whatever happens. It affirms that deep down, life is good, no matter what. It's not to be confused with simple optimism, which says that no matter what life will be great. Optimistic people are known to see only part of the picture, the part they like. Rarely have I met optimistic parents. The realities of parenthood seem to erode any worldview that everything is "just wonderful." But parents with hope? Yes, there are many. And when married couples decide to have a child, their decision will often be seasoned with hope.

Besides the virtue of hope, the decision to parent may also include an assessment of the world's condition. After all, you're inviting someone to live in it. Social philosophers and politicians offer a variety of descriptions on the state of the world. You may have noticed that there's not necessarily agreement among them.

To risk oversimplification, we might divide their assessment into two camps. The first group favors a message that the powers of evil are winning. To survive we must relentlessly fight for our existence. Life during these challenging times is basically a knock-down, drag-out battle between the forces of good and evil. In such a situation we best live with heightened vigilance and fear. Those on this side claim to be realists and offer us the daily newspaper and the evening television news as proof of their position.

On the other side of this debate are those who admit the presence of evil and potential harm, but at the same time, replace fear with hope, and even love. They view life as more of a gift than a struggle. Great and wonderful events happen every day. Each day is another opportunity to make things better than they were the day before. In the end, goodness will prevail. It will be a challenge, but the world is tilted toward the good.[2]

Basic values and attitudes can and should influence us when it comes to making a decision about whether to parent. This is no time for naive thinking. To become a parent is easily among the most important decisions we make in our lives. I believe that the decision to have a child requires no small amount of courage. We need courage when we first decide to have a child and in all subsequent decisions about that child and when we decide to have more. All acts of genuine creation include courage because we move from the known to the unknown, the "what never was" to "what will be." Courage is especially important in changing times because many of the old supports for living appear to be weakening. It's scary because it's like exploring new territory without a map. So deciding to procreate needs genuine courage.[3]

The Catholic Church has valued parenting as central to marriage. Vatican II captured this dimension of marriage in the following.

---

[2] See Michael Lerner, *The Left Hand of God: Taking Back Our Country From the Religious Right* (San Francisco: HarperSanFrancisco, 2006).

[3] An excellent description of the need for courage can be found in Rollo May, *The Courage to Create* (New York: W. W. Norton and Company, 1975).

Marriage and married love are by nature ordered to the procreation and education of children. Indeed children are the supreme gift of marriage and greatly contribute to the well-being of parents themselves. God said, 'It is not good that man should live alone' (Gen 2:18), and from the beginning (God) made them male and female.' (Mt 9:14); wishing to associate them in a special way with his own creative work, God blessed the man and woman with the words: 'Be fruitful and multiply' (Gen 1:28). Without intending to underestimate the other ends of marriage, it must be said that true married love and the family life that flows from it has this end in view: that the spouses would cooperate generously with the love of the Creator and Savior, who through them in due time increase and enrich his family.[4]

Far from the language of burdensome responsibility, the church points to the many positive aspects of having children, not the least of which is free and active cooperation with God as Creator in bringing new life into the world. What's also worth emphasizing is that children themselves are a wondrous expression of marital love. At the deepest level of God's creation, and in accord with God's own dream for creation, all authentic human love generates life. When it comes to marriage, both generous divine and human love are sealed together as the source of new life.

And a word should be added about the deep joy that parenting can bring. I can share hundreds of moments when I felt more alive in the knowledge and observation of our children, five of whom came to us the usual way and two by adoption. Most are on their own starting their own families. Some remain with us at home. I take particular delight when they all "come home." I can experience such deep feelings of profound satisfaction and joy just through watching them interact with each other and with their mother and me. When I look at each one I don't see dollar signs but signs of life painted in so many colors of the rainbow. We have a family custom of having what we call "a slide night." That means I drag out shoe boxes filled with photographic slides taken over the years, mostly of our children. In the next life, I will sort and catalog my collection, but for now it's all random. A picture taken near the birth of one is followed by a prom picture of another with his or her date. Every slide receives raucous laughter and abundant comment about the clothing styles of the time and something along the line of "that was the

---

[4] Vatican II, The Pastoral Constitution on the Church in the Modern World, 50.

time when so-and-so wet his pants." It can get pretty earthy, but yet, oh so wonderful! As an aside, we have found that exposing our collection to would-be spouses of our children is one of the best forms of marriage preparation. Both the pictures and the accompanying family script give as much information as does any premarriage questionnaire. So, despite the negatives we often hear about parenting, there are a million positives which will be unique to each family.

So love is there in fullness as the couple expresses their love for each other in total sexual union, an act so fitting as the complete gift of self that constitutes Christian marriage. But it's also there as the foundation of their parenting once a child is born. Anything less than this love deprives the world of one of its greatest happenings, the generous sharing of loving persons in creating new life.[5]

Before laying the groundwork for a spiritual understanding of parenting, I want to add some thoughts about the Catholic Church and its approach to artificial contraception. I do this with awareness that the church's teaching in this matter has been a source of debate and disagreement among Catholics for many years.

First, it's inaccurate to say that the Catholic Church is totally against birth control. For many years, the church has advocated "responsible parenthood," meaning that the couple is responsible for deciding when to have children, how they might be spaced, and how many children to have. Issues of health, economics, and the needs of already existing children are all to be considered as the couple makes decisions. Also, the general condition of society should also be included in their discernment of what's best to do in their particular situation. So there's no debate in the church that the decision to have children has moral and personal implications.

The debate concerns what method should the couple use to actualize this responsibility. There are chemical ways to alter the woman's fertility cycle. There are also so-called barrier methods that prevent the sperm and ovum from uniting. There are also medical ways to render either the man or the woman infertile, temporarily or permanently. The Catholic Church, in general, considers all these methods "unnatural" or not in accord with our biological nature as God created us. In various ways, they are seen as blocking God's intent for the full expression of love in sexual intercourse, which must remain open to creating new life. The

---

[5] For how becoming a parent invites a new way of loving, see Lauren Slater, *Love Works Like This: Moving from One Kind of Life to Another* (New York: Random House, 2002).

landmark papal document in recent times that dealt with this noted the following.

> These acts, by which husband and wife are united in chaste intimacy, and by means of which human life is transmitted, are as the Council (Vatican II) recalled 'noble and worthy,' and they do not cease to be lawful if, independent of the will of husband and wife, they are foreseen to be infertile, since they always remain ordained toward expressing and consolidating their union. . . . God has wisely disposed natural laws and rhythms of fecundity which, of themselves, cause a succession of births. Nevertheless the Church, calling men back to the observance of the norms of natural law, as interpreted by their constant doctrine, teaches that each and every marriage act must remain open to the transmission of life.[6]

Pope John Paul II, in his many addresses and writings, maintained this teaching and focused especially on the marital act as expressing the full gift of self to another. He judged the various forms of contraception as compromising or limiting the full openness between husband and wife, which included an openness to new life. Here is a sampling of his thinking.

> When couples, by means of recourse to contraception, separate these two meanings (unitive and procreative) that God the creator has inscribed in the being of man and woman and in the dynamism of their sexual communion, they act as 'arbiters' of the divine plan and they 'manipulate' and degrade human sexuality and with it themselves and their married partner by altering its value of 'total self-giving.' Thus the language that expresses the total reciprocal self-giving of husband and wife is overlaid, through contraception, by objectively contradictory language, namely, that of not giving oneself totally to the other.[7]

In accord with his personalistic approach to marriage and sexuality, the Pope highlights that loving sexual intercourse is designed by God to express something quite specific: total mutual self-giving. While accepting the traditional approach to this topic in natural law, he makes a significant contribution to this topic by focusing on the dignity of the

---

[6] Pope Paul VI, *Humanae Vitae* (On Human Life), 11.
[7] Pope John Paul II, *Familiaris Consortio* (On the Family), 32.

human person, which was a major theme during his long pontificate. Many find this approach prophetic in the face of how so many cultures denigrate or trivialize human sexuality both inside and outside marriage. His approach is also connected with his important teachings on the culture of life. The Pope offered his reflections on human sexuality in a series of addresses early in his pontificate gathered together and titled *The Theology of the Body*.[8]

The Catholic Church is quite concerned that married couples make all their important and far-reaching decisions within marriage in light of the Gospels and the teachings of the church. Much effort has been put into this ministry of education and support to the married, especially as couples are preparing for marriage. Both at the local parish level and at the diocesan level excellent programs now exist, given by informed and trained Catholics, many of whom are married. Often this training includes education in the practice of Natural Family Planning, which is based on the most recent research in fertility awareness. Using NFP, as it's often called, demands understanding and personal discipline. With this method being "natural," it offers the additional benefit of not introducing potentially harmful chemicals into the body. In other words, it is "environmentally safe," which is no small value in our world today.

As I've said already, our focus here is on Christian marriage itself and its procreative or generative aspect. Our theological foundation arises from a deep understanding of God's creative love, which by its very nature, creates new life. And those of us called to create this way receive both our call and our capability directly from God. Every child born into this world is, first of all, a gift from God. Not simply as some would have it, a surprise or even a blessing, although it may be that too. God is the first author of life. Today we are helped in grasping this wonderful spiritual truth by contemporary science, which is resolutely sketching the almost incredible set of cosmic circumstances that have created the specific conditions where life first came into being and, then after the passage of many years of almost unbelievable changes, human life come into being on Planet Earth. What an awesome responsibility we accept when we open our lives to continue this miraculous process.[9]

[8] Pope John Paul II, *The Theology of the Body: Human Love in the Divine Plan* (Boston: Pauline Books and Media, 1997).

[9] A fine overview of this aspect of parenting is found in J. Bradley Wigger, *The Power of God at Home: Nurturing Our Children in Love and Grace* (San Francisco: Jossey-Bass, 2003).

The ministry of co-creating with God

Before discussing the specifics of Christian parenting, I want to sketch a broad understanding of "life in general" for all of us. I believe that such a move will help us to appreciate more fully the meaning and importance of what we do when, through parenting, we assist our children in becoming persons created in God's image. There's a story going around these days about two stonecutters who were charged with fashioning stones for a local project in their town. When asked what they were doing, one simply noted that he was cutting stone. The other, however, smiled and responded that he was building a cathedral that he hoped would last forever. Obviously the latter felt his work to be important and meaningful because he saw the fuller meaning of his effort. I would like to do something similar here in sharing some ideas of how parenting fits into the larger context of assisting in God's work of creation.

Like many others, I grew up with an understanding that this world was like a stage, where the characters and the script were a given. The whole shebang was created by God and each of us only had to learn our part and begin. I believed that my life, and everyone else's for that matter, was mostly like a scripted stage play in which each of us takes turns in playing our part for our allotted time. Shakespeare liked to use that image.

Mostly this meant that our task was to fit into an already existing plan. Once we did, we just let our lives unfold. The old phrase that "nothing new is created under the sun" served as part of this understanding. For instance, as a youngster in Catholic school, I learned that God had vocational plans for each of us. Being a boy, there were basically two options placed before me: priesthood or marriage. I also believed that part of my eternal destiny was determined by my faithful response to what God intended for me. I had to find the appropriate state in life that corresponded to my calling. Vocation was a very big word in those days. It still is, but its meaning today is a little broader.

Priests and nuns back then were heavily into recruiting. Early on, I learned that my academic performance in the judgment of my teachers might receive a more generous appraisal if they thought I might be heading for the seminary. So it wasn't a bad idea to show some early interest. Eventually, I did enter the seminary and religious life and stayed with it for eight years until my religious superiors convinced me that, at least back then, I lacked certain essential qualities for ordination. With the help of a very good spiritual director I came to see that they were right and that I would move from one state in life to another, namely "the lay state."

But something else was changing within me. I began to see human life in more dynamic terms. I began to think about life differently. For instance, my entrance into the seminary was not a mistake. My eight years there were a time of deep learning and personal growth. This brought me to think that there was a rich variety of life paths. I began to wonder about how much of life was preordained by God and how much resulted from our free decisions.

Gradually I began to see my life, and everyone else's, not so much as the unfolding of a preexisting plot, but as an evolving drama that was more like the kind of stage performance where maybe the first line is given and the actors proceed to make it up the rest of the way. To use a musical analogy, life is more like spontaneous jazz than playing each and every note of Beethoven's Fifth.

As I studied theology both as a formal academic discipline and as a way of learning more about the life that God has so wonderfully and mysteriously crafted for each of us, I was drawn to a view of creation that was quite different from the one I'd had in my earlier years. I began to think that God's creation is not fixed or finished. It's more a work in progress. I found great insight in the theological work of process theologians, both Catholic and Protestant. I was particularly drawn to the thought of Teilhard de Chardin, the great Jesuit scientist and theologian. I also began to see a deep connection between theology and spirituality.

As an example of how this new process approach to life works, let's reflect on what I am doing at this moment as I write these words. They are mine and they are absolutely new. While there's always a possibility of a certain duplication, my guess is that the thoughts I am having, the words that I use to express them, the precise order of words I am selecting have never come into being quite this way in the entire history of the universe. They are, I would hope, part of what St. Paul called "the new creation."

But that can be said about so much of what each of us does each day, unless we have fallen into a hopeless routine of sameness. Recall the myth of Sisyphus where that poor fellow was stuck pushing that rock up the hill over and over again without ever reaching the top. I know we all have days like that, but on the whole, let's pray for progress. And variety. We have been vested with the gift of freedom and creativity. Why not use these gifts as often as possible?

We have all been invited to participate in a grand project that began when God said over the formless void and the darkness that spread over the deep, "Let there be light."[10] And the lights began to go on virtually everywhere as stellar nuclear furnaces ignited in a billion places throughout the universe. Jesus took the meaning of light a step further by inviting us to turn on the light within each of us, the divine spark that animates our being. In part, he was pointing to the light of God's life in our intelligence and the light of life in our heart.

Toward the end of his brilliant treatise on human evolution, Teilhard de Chardin writes the following.

> How can we fail to see that after having centered each one of us, both you and me, individually on ourselves, it is forever the same cyclone (but this time on a social scale) that continues its advance overhead, drawing us all tighter together in an embrace that tends to perfect each one of us as it binds us organically to all others at once.[11]

As a scientist and mystic Teilhard saw the world as moving through space and time, empowered by God's Spirit and energized by human effort. In a sense, within the whole of humankind he perceived two specific movements that characterized the present flow of love. The first advanced inward creating in us a deeper consciousness of ourselves and the world around us. Through this move we accepted and savored our uniqueness. We came into ever-deepening knowledge of our identity. Obviously, this process is ongoing and knows no end since at our deepest point, we are connected with the unfathomable mystery of God.

Commensurately with the inward process is one that escorts us outside ourselves as we connect with others through love. Teilhard will name this "convergence." The effect of coming together builds not just those directly involved, but quietly yet resolutely builds the entire universe. Teilhard would never be accused of thinking small. What's important is to acknowledge the gains made through acts of love. They occur in three contexts.

First, we affirm growth in the individual person who advances in human life through an interior transformation which Teilhard would also affirm is the work of God. His writings often note how we are

---

[10] Gen 1:3.

[11] Pierre Teilhard de Chardin, *The Human Phenomenon*, trans. Sarah Appleton-Weber (Brighton: Sussex Academic Press, 1999) 220.

collaborators, coworkers or cocreators with God in the overall work of developing creation, especially our own.

Second, there is expansion in the concrete social units involved in the act of love, where life is shared, supported, and nurtured. Imagine that growth as creation advancing. The world of close interpersonal life is one of the most fertile settings for the New Creation to unfold. Note all the times that Jesus focused his attention and care upon individuals: the woman at the well, the paralyzed person who was lowered through the roof, Peter's mother-in-law, the man born blind, and, of course, Mary Magdalene.

And finally, the contribution of love should be expanded to be part of the spiritual wealth of all humankind, adding to the great work of building up the universe as a place of freedom, awareness, and love. All of this is incorporated in Teilhard, who understood the work of Christ as goal of all creation. He called it the work of the Cosmic Christ. Obviously, we can only offer a sampling of his overall vision. And we must affirm, too, that Teilhard does not stand alone in such imaginings, even though he came to his perception of creation many decades ago.[12]

With this more dynamic understanding of God's creation, we can now apply this to the ministry of parenting. Through parenting we directly assist others especially as they begin their own spiritual journey to God. We are placed by God in a position of maximum influence, especially in our children's early years.

The sacred ministry of parents

Having taken a little side trip into the world of speculative theology, let's return to the specific topic of Christian parenting. What happens is that the general intent of God for creating life from love is focused within the family where human life first comes into being and is developed, especially during the highly vulnerable early years. Recall that the church has taught that one goal of marriage is the procreation and education of children. I like to think of education in accord with the root meaning of the Latin word which means, "to lead out."

Parents are the first to introduce their children to the wonders of God's world. They are the first to preach the Good News to their children.

---

[12] An excellent introduction to his thought can be found in Ursula King, *Spirit of Fire: The Life and Vision of Teilhard de Chardin* (Maryknoll: Orbis Books, 1996).

They are the first to show children the way of life that was taught by Jesus. They are the first to offer the most wonderful and important of all human experiences, that of being accepted, cherished, and loved. They "lead out" their children by encouragement and example. And when does this responsibility end? I'm not sure. I do know that my dad was still telling me how to drive when he was in his nineties![13]

Here is another sampling of the words of Pope John Paul II relating to this sacred parental task. "The task of giving education is rooted in the primary vocation of married couples to participate in God's creative activity. By begetting in love and for love a new person who has within himself or herself the vocation for growth and development, parents by that very fact take the task of that person effectively to live a fully human life."[14]

In our day we witness abundant parental concern and involvement in the development of children. We also sadly know of situations of parental abuse and neglect. But let's stay positive because that's part of the picture, too. Not only does parental interest include good formal education, but also a series of what are called extracurricular educational opportunities that prepare the child for competency in athletics, music, art, and whatever is being offered in local communities for children. Some parenting experts wonder whether some children might be over-scheduled and have too much to deal with. Without moments of silence, rest, and just "chilling out," as is now said, their deeper growth as persons may be actually diminished. It's certainly worth thinking about, especially when we think of raising our children (and ourselves as parents) in a spiritual milieu.[15]

Parenting also demands a complex calculation of the appropriate kind of distance to create in the parent-child relationship. After all, most parents are fully in favor of their children leaving home to fend for themselves.

Most know that the first two years of life involve extreme closeness between the parent and child. Parenthetically, parenting should also involve fathers. Gradually, the amount of closeness, especially at the

[13] For a fuller understanding of the interpersonal dynamics operative in the first years of life, see T. Barry Brazelton and Bertrand G. Cramer, *The Earliest Relationship: Parents, Infants and the Drama of Early Attachment* (New York: Addison-Wesley Publishing Co., 1990).

[14] Pope John Paul II, *Familiaris Consortio* (On the Family) 36.

[15] See a most creative approach to this dimension of parenting in David Spangler, *Parent as Mystic, Mystic as Parent* (New York: Riverhead Books, 1998).

physical level, will decrease although personal and spiritual connections need to remain consistent and strong. This is especially important during the teen years when this matter can seem like a tug-of-war as the adolescent seeks more freedom and independence.

Hard and fast rules about the exact amount of space to maintain between parents and children are impossible to make and dangerous to even want. Parents and children are unique beings, and circumstances change by the minute. But some degree of togetherness is necessary.

Many family experts warn that the role of parents is often usurped by the culture, especially through the media. They advise parents to be vigilant about what's happening in the subcultures of young people, especially teens. Having gone through this situation more than once, I can share that "their" culture will often appear distorted, dangerous, and even demented. When parents become exposed to the various elements in their world, really listen to their music, read their magazines, attend their concerts and the like, it can seem like visiting a foreign country, even a distant planet. But acquaintance with their world helps the parent to remain in closer touch with children during a time in their lives when they are most vulnerable to some pretty dangerous situations.[16]

Despite what we see in the newspapers and television these days, there are some very good aspects of parenting worth mentioning. Many parents are deeply committed and conscientious about their role as parents. They attend school meetings, watch Little League sports events in which their children are playing, and they attend every band concert in which their child sits with an instrument that is almost larger than the child. In reality, the music may be terrible, but most parents won't say that. Their comment would be that it was as good as what's offered at Carnegie Hall and, for them, that's true.

Their love for their children is boundless. They will sacrifice mightily so that the child receives all that's needed. They will give up time and money for their child's sake and not think twice about whether it's worth it. They will do anything to stay close to their children, like listening to what happened at school that day with the fullest degree of attention, even though they heard the exact same recounting two days before. They

---

[16] A family expert who is most articulate in describing this is Mary Pipher. See Mary Pipher, *The Shelter of Each Other: Rebuilding Our Families* (New York: G. P. Putnam Sons, 1998) and Mary Pipher, *Reviving Ophelia: Saving the Selves of Adolescent Girls* (New York: Ballantine Books, 1994).

will lose sleep worrying about their kid's grades, friends, and problems, yet they will thank God daily for the experience of being a parent. I know that I am painting this picture with bright colors and I know, as well as any parent, that there are moments when we are broken apart by what's required of us, especially during tough times. I readily agree with those who confess that nothing can be more demanding or more difficult than being a good parent.

But that's not a bad thing. Often when we face difficulties, when we are at the end of our rope, that's when our humanity grows the most. Love can break open our hearts as we face parental challenges. With open hearts, there is more room for life, for others, and for God. While in the middle of some mess with our children, parents may long to be on some cruise ship visiting beautiful Caribbean islands, but when we come to our senses, we give thanks for being there, as we say, "for them." In fact, it's during such moments of challenge and difficulty that our personal sanctity as parents develops.

Unfortunately, we don't seem to have many models of good parenting even in the life of the church. Or even much of an awareness of the importance of the vocation of Christian parenting. The Catholic Church has a way of affirming goodness and holiness through its practice of canonizing saints. During his pontificate Pope John Paul II made over three hundred new saints.

But were any of them canonized because they were exceptional parents? Or, to refer to the main topic of this book, were they named saints because they were exemplary married persons? I don't think so. There was one couple from Italy that "made it" but their cause was advanced, it was noted, because all their children entered the religious life or the priesthood. In fact, it was reported that they ceased intimate relations in their marriage with the birth of their last child. I'm not making a judgment on their sanctity. I've already mentioned that we are each unique as we walk our spiritual path. But it would be helpful, I would think, if our awareness of the basic holiness of parenting was more available, more real, for most parents. When we pray for vocations during Mass, are we, as a church, thinking of parents? Probably not.

The family is rarely a smoothly functioning social unit. Instead of monastic silence, there is the noise of the TV set, the ringing of phones, the sound of video games, the chatter of kid's talk, and even the occasional slamming of doors. Is this the sound of holiness? Sometimes, I believe, it is exactly that. It is out of the moments of noise and mess, and occasionally unbearable silence, that the church of the home, the domestic church as it's referred to in current church parlance, is created and formed.[17]

Because parenting includes basically everything happening between parent and child, each day, the range of Christian parenting includes a lot. The focus of parenting is the totality of what constitutes human life. Plus, anything connected with the practical life of love. I have always treasured the words of Rosemary Haughton, a mother and a theologian, who wrote years ago, "The purpose of the family is for the formation of people who are able to love."[18]

I would assume that such an understanding of family life applies to both children and parents. Think about it: the ability to love. What is more basic and more important than that? Are not our lives of love the very essence of Christian spirituality? And when it comes to family life, are not the actions of love so very ordinary? And is this not the challenge for all of us who seek to live a fully spiritual life when we are married and with children? On the surface, our lives appear completely ordinary. Nothing special. Just getting food on the table, clothes on our bodies, and a roof over our heads. What's more ordinary than that? Well, I suspect you know where this is leading us, right to the story of the final judgment in St. Matthew's Gospel. Whatever you did for the least, which may be a reference to those we are with every day, you did for me.

Parents are conduits for God's love touching their children. Sometimes parents are also blessed by experiencing a sort of round-trip of love, when children return the love they have received. It's all part of God's magnificent design. The role of parents is in many ways irreplaceable. The church has recognized this.

Even in the secular arena, the significance of parents is being recognized. While the debate over "family values" has many complexities and even some inconsistencies, one thing is agreed on by all: all children do best when they are loved and valued by their parents.

Pope John Paul II taught that one of the most important tasks of the family was its service or ministry to life. No other social institution was closer to the issues of life and death than was the family. In that spirit he saw that the family was positioned in society to not only serve the lives of children who entered the family through the usual expressions

---

[17] See a wonderful account of this kind of spirituality in Patricia H. Livingston, *This Blessed Mess: Finding Hope Amidst Life's Chaos* (Notre Dame: Sorin Books, 2000).

[18] Rosemary Haughton, *Problems of Christian Marriage* (New York: Paulist Press, 1968) 21.

of marital love, but also those children who, through a variety of circumstances, entered the life of the family through other ways. The family was to be a home where hospitality was offered to all.

Our own family has experienced the blessings of adoption and caring for foster children. I feel drawn to mention this dimension of parenting because it is so important in today's less than perfect society. All married couples are called to the generous sharing of their love. Some will never have their own children, but they will express generative love in other ways, like in the care of children who are poor, challenged physically or mentally, or those who simply need a big brother or sister. Some will decide to foster or adopt children. One of the most powerful expressions of this is found in those who travel to the far ends of the earth to adopt children in need of families.

In all these ways, they "serve life," to use the words of Pope John Paul II. He writes, "Christian families will show greater readiness to adopt and foster children who have lost their parents or have been abandoned by them."[19] He sees for these children the possibility of rediscovering God's love in a special way through the acceptance, warmth, and affection of a family. His own love for children was demonstrated over and over again on his travels. In a sense, as a young man in his early twenties, he, himself, felt the pain of being an orphan having lost his mother, father, and a brother.

Beneath all that we have discussed about marriage and family life flows a rich spirituality, a presence of God that is as real as the ground we stand on. I have recently found a wonderful image to direct our attention to this important, but often unacknowledged spiritual presence. The earth that we see is covered by a crust of rock with large pockets of water called oceans. But if we dig toward the center of our planet, we will soon encounter molten rock, what geologists call the magma. It is in liquid form and very hot. We witness its presence in volcanic eruptions when it tunnels through the crust layer and reaches the surface. The magma is right below us wherever we are, but rarely if ever are we conscious of it.

The spiritual dimension of life is a lot like that, present everywhere, but often unrecognized and missed. In recent years, however, more and more married couples have reflected upon their lives and discovered (although it was always there) a profound spiritual dimension to married life. We'll highlight some of their findings in the next chapter.

---

[19] Pope John Paul II, *Familiaris Consortio* (On the Family) 41.

Chapter Seven

What's spiritual about marriage?

When I married many years ago, I was, as some say, on the rebound. After graduating from high school, I felt that I was called by God to enter a religious community and eventually become a Catholic priest. I gave it my best shot, but it wasn't enough. After eight years in the seminary, I was asked to reconsider my vocational direction by my religious superiors, and after some honest and deep assessment, I decided that my call was elsewhere.

After "leaving" (the parlance of the day), I married and soon thereafter children began to push out the walls of our small home. Through all these years, however adequate or inadequate my effort, I sought to live a spiritual life, first as a vowed religious, and later as a married layperson and parent. I wanted to learn how to be more connected with God through it all. My eventual decision to seek further education in the theology of marriage and family life flowed in part from my desire to understand and grow closer to God as I lived my quite ordinary, daily life. I don't want this to sound overly pious or heroic. But like everyone, I felt this was my one shot at a good life, so I didn't want to waste it.

I soon learned that there wasn't much of a conversation going on in the church about marital spirituality. I recall visiting a well-stocked Catholic bookstore and among the fifty or so books they carried dealing with spirituality, not a single one was about married life. Not even a chapter! I know now that this dearth of published material has changed a little as more married persons have become trained theologians and spiritual writers. Most consultations with the laity in the church also reveal high interest in spiritual growth. Published accounts of marital spirituality are certainly on the rise.[1]

Most worthwhile these days is the work of the International Academy for Marital Spirituality (INTAMS), located in Belgium, which has produced over the years an outstanding journal on this topic as well as sponsored various educational events. This institute of reflection, research, and learning has almost single-handedly brought this topic to the table of academic and theological conversation. Yet there remains much room for further growth.

Recently, I was invited by a diocese in California to offer a retreat to married couples. I always welcome such invitations. Discussing with others what's of central importance to oneself is about as good as it gets. At our first meeting, I conducted a brief survey of the group concerning their understanding and awareness of what's spiritual about their marriages. I asked them to list the top three experiences in their marriages when they felt closest to God. I collected their responses and totaled them to share in the next session.

I had done this before, so I was not surprised at what they reported. In general, the most spiritual time mentioned was associated with the birth of their children. Second, they usually recalled something having to do with the sacramental life of the church, like attending Mass together. And third, they described times involving prayer, either said individually or as a couple. All of these experiences are good and certainly deserve mentioning. Involvement in the sacramental life of the church and regular prayer are important for all those seeking to find God in our increasingly secular culture. But I had to ask myself, what about the experience of marriage itself? Were there any rich spiritual moments that came directly from their loving relationship as married persons?

What I, as others, describe as what might be called moments of spiritual awareness, too often people think primarily about *religious* activities, and not about ordinary human experiences that might be crammed, though unnoticed, with God's presence. Clearly, I was happy to see that many sensed God within the experience of the birth of a child, but what about all the rest? Didn't people see the powerful connection between the act of marital love and the love of God? I'm not sure.

---

[1] See a comprehensive listing of this in Monica Sandor, "Contemporary Marital Spirituality: A Survey of the Principal Themes," *INTAMS review*, Autumn (2005) 238–55.

What follows in this chapter's description of marital spirituality is something old and something new. The old part is a framework that I have chosen for this presentation of the spiritual dimension of marriage. Many Catholics in the United States will recognize the answer that was given to one of the first questions in the old Baltimore Catechism. It has to do with the question of why we have been created. In a sense, of course, the question is timeless. Part of the answer, memorized by literally millions of Catholics over the years was this: "To know, love, and serve God." Knowledge of God, along with all that was connected with God, challenged the mind. Love of God, and all that was connected with God's love, challenged the heart. Serving God, and all that God cared about, challenged what one did. A shortened form of the same formula was that our Christian life involved head, heart, and hands.

The new part of this chapter will connect this formula with a wide-ranging and helpful description of marital spirituality. I'll begin with a reflection on the life of the mind or how we think about spirituality in connection with married life. Special attention will be given to our being fully present to each other. Following that, I'll focus on love, the center or driving force of marital spirituality, by connecting love of God with marital love. And I'll conclude with the importance of expressing love in concrete actions that enrich the daily lives of married Christians.

I firmly believe that there is a distinct spirituality for the married. And I do not stand alone in this. While not developed in great detail, there exists a consistent papal paper trail advocating marital spirituality. I call to mind the words of Pope Pius XI written in 1930 when he said referring to Christian marriage: "This mutual inward molding of husband and wife, this determined effort to perfect each other, can in a real sense, as the Roman Catechism teaches, be said to be the chief reason and purpose of matrimony."[2] We can also add these wonderful words of Pope Paul VI in an address to married couples belonging to the Teams of Our Lady, an association dedicated primarily to support spirituality in marriage. "Like all who are baptized, you are, in fact, called to holiness. . . . But you should pursue this objective in your own manner, in and through your life as couples."[3] These papal words find echo in the words of Vatican II, when describing the universal call to holiness, they

---

[2] Pope Pius XI, *Casti Connubii* (On Christian Marriage), December 31, 1930, section 50.

[3] Pope Paul VI, "Address to the Teams of Our Lady," May 1, 1970, section 1.

specifically address married couples to "follow their own proper path to holiness."[4]

Implied in all these statements is the claim that a spirituality for the married will contain distinctive characteristics that will differ in some degree with the spirituality of those unmarried. Our task here will be to single out some of its features.

Awareness of sacred presence

Let's start with a simple illustration from the natural world. The earth is surrounded by a thin layer of life-supporting, gaseous elements. They are largely invisible and mostly unnoticed, unless, of course, they are contaminated by toxic substances or when they rapidly move, causing us to declare it is truly a blustery day. We also know that these airy chemicals support our lives especially by providing the oxygen needed for creating and sustaining the biological processes required for human life. Put simply, no air, no life, at least as we understand this phenomenon from where we stand on our gorgeous blue planet. Yet we mostly pass our time blithely unaware of our essential need for it.

Something similar to this can be said about God's presence with us as creatures dwelling on the earth. Often, the divine presence is unnoticed because of its so-called spiritual dimension. Though imperceptible, God is omnipresent in creation. According to philosophers and theologians, God is the ultimate explanation of "why there is something instead of nothing." God has been described as the first cause of all that is and the final direction of where everything is headed. There are countless ways to describe this spiritual dimension of reality, and many names are given to it by various religions and cultures.

It is generally held that the very existence of creation requires some kind of transcendent presence with exceedingly abundant power. If we imagine creation as coming from nothing at all, we're talking about rather remarkable power. This divine reality is commonly believed to have no beginning or end. It is timeless and eternal. How did God get to be God? No one I know can say. St. Thomas Aquinas taught that God was "an uncaused cause."

---

[4] Vatican II, *Lumen Gentium* (The Dogmatic Constitution on the Church), section 41.

I think it's important to begin our discussion of the spiritual dimension of marital experience with some broad strokes on the canvas of creation relating to spiritual awareness and the "place" of God in our life. While marital spirituality is something in its own right, it remains a part of the spirituality shared by all. It participates in that wondrous search to find God in all things created.[5] It includes distinctive traits because of the nature of marriage itself. Yet the specific ways we live, like a powerful magnet, draw only certain parts of God's creation into themselves. Marriage is no exception.

So let's start by affirming that God is everywhere and in everything. God is the before, the middle, and the end. God is larger than all creation (which today some scientists argue may include billions of universes—if God can do one, why not more?). God is also present within all creation, particularly within those who bear God's image. That means all of us!

In the Christian worldview, this divine presence is called "God" or "the Trinity" or "Father" or, as St. John notes in one of his epistles, simply "Love." Right away, we do well to begin our reflection on marital spirituality by thinking about God in all-encompassing relational terms. God's own interior life is relational. Again, many "names" have been used to capture this profound truth, the most common being Father, Son, and Holy Spirit. But other ways of describing the same truth are Creator, Redeemer, and Sanctifier, or Lover, the Beloved, and the Love-Between-Them. The key idea always being that, within God, divine life is constant and eternal divine loving. The image of God sitting upon a heavenly throne can be deceiving. In my view there's not enough action in such a view. It appears too sterile and sedate. From all we know about God, which admittedly isn't the whole picture, God is quite active and involved. In a word, God is the most alive and most loving reality that is! God never sits on a rocking chair doing nothing.

What else might we say about God? Most of what we know that's worthwhile about the nature or personality of God comes from the person, the deeds, and the words of Jesus Christ, who himself was God's Son. He possessed both the identity of being God and of being human. This belief, called the Mystery of the Incarnation, says that about two thousand years ago, in our time and place of earth, God chose to become present as a human being. Using images and words drawn from St. John's Gospel, God did this in part to show us, in Jesus, the truth of what God is like

---

[5] For a helpful account of how this can be done today, see Gerard Hughes, *God in All Things* (London: Hodder and Stoughton, 2003).

and how we can best live the human life that we've been gifted with. Two messages, so to speak, at the same time. But both messages say something quite similar. To be God is to love. To be human is to do the same.

With these two magnificent foundation stones of faith we can begin to trace a kind of map for marital spirituality. First, God is immediately present to all creation and especially to human life. That means God is present within marriage. I find it helpful to think of God dwelling in the space between the husband and wife.

And, second, we are connected to God's presence primarily through marital love, through the thousands of acts of love expressed in daily marital life. As we love each other, we are also loving God. We talked about this in an earlier chapter, but it is well worth repeating. Marital spirituality is daily enriched by loving gestures as ordinary as taking out the garbage or going to pick up ice cream from the store, two acts that happened in my married life just today. Nothing is too mundane or menial to exclude from the spiritual life of the married. But are we sufficiently aware of God in such common activities? Here may be a way to help us gain greater awareness in these matters.

First, I believe we have to have some sense of the reality we are searching for. God's presence is subtle, to say the least. Sort of behind what's in front of us. Here's a suggestion. Focus on being more present to this moment as you're reading this. Begin, by being present to yourself. A common practice used in presentations about any spirituality is to first have those assembled seek a state of being quiet. Set aside notebooks and reading material. Fold your hands in your lap. And breathe. Yes, focus your attention on the simple act of breathing. Breathe in, and draw a sense of life from the outside. Breathe out, and send your life moving outward. In and out, from and to, received and given forth. There are many ways to do this exercise. And they are mostly quite effective. The whole intent is to awaken us to something we so easily take for granted, the very act of being alive.

How many hours, even days pass by without our conscious awareness that we are here, right now, pulsating with vitality in a once-in-a-lifetime moment? It's said we are much too externally-referenced people. That means that we're attentive to our external environment, but virtually oblivious to what's happening inside us. The beginning of spiritual awareness involves an awareness of our own interior self. That's often a challenge in itself.

I recall talking recently with a teacher of young children. She liked to have her students spend a little time each day just sitting quietly in silence. She invited them to make a short visit inside themselves. Obedient as most little ones are, she said they would all close their eyes and journey inward—or at least, attempt to do so. After doing this brief activity for a few days, she started to notice a little agitation on the part of some students. As good teachers do when questions arise, she inquired of those who seemed to feel uncomfortable with the exercise. Most of them said the same thing: They felt they had no inside to visit. Their entire world was on the outside. Welcome to the universe of 24-hour broadcasting, portable music systems, and constant noise.

Perhaps many of us might have difficulty dwelling within ourselves. We may find silence to be an uncomfortable place to be. And if one cannot sense being present to oneself, how might we do so with others? This is well worth reflecting on.

Let's assume, however, that we have learned the art of self-reflection and enjoy many moments each day of simple awareness of our own being. The next step would be to create a similar consciousness or awareness of our neighbor. Given our present topic, this would lead us to attend more fully to the presence of our husband or wife. Obviously, we would try to focus on their personal presence, which extends well beyond their role, their gender, their appearance, their age, and so forth.

Genuine interpersonal presence can be as illusive as is awareness of our own presence. So many of our daily responses to each other are more or less automatic or pre-programmed. We often fly on autopilot. Especially with those we live with or meet every day. I'm thinking now of the important insights of Martin Buber and his advocacy of the I-Thou encounter. Achieving this type of encounter requires no small amount of personal discipline. We have to create in ourselves a capacity for deep interpersonal receptivity and response. We seek a presence filled with both the self and the other. I would hope that a richly spiritual marital life would seek and include many sacred moments of deep interpersonal encounter. And if we were fully attentive, would not such moments provide at least some glimmer of the presence of God as one fully available, receptive, and loving?[6]

This description of interpersonal moments within marriage also reminds us that the encounter must be fully mutual. Certainly we can sense that this goal is no small challenge. It requires not one well-disposed

---

[6] Martin Buber, *I and Thou* (New York: Charles Scribner's Sons, 1970). See also Joe McGowen, *Availability: Gabriel Marcel and the Phenomenology of Human Openness* (Missoula, MT: Scholars Press, 1978).

person, but two. And in the case of marriage, the two persons are not at all carbon copies of each other. They bear gender differences in every cell of their bodies. Their brains, we are now told, work differently. They communicate through different styles and structures. To use a current image, they each come from different planets. And of course, each one carries within himself and herself the accumulated history of each one's life up to that moment. And yet we dare to hope that they are to connect at the deepest level of personhood? Sounds a bit daunting, doesn't it? But that's part of the miracle of creation and of God's intent for marriage.

I also think that it's helpful to remember that marriage has been graced and empowered by God for this sacred work. The stage has been set. The curtain has been raised. All is readied by God's Spirit, yet, to tell the whole story, one matter is wanting. Our individual, personal response. So well is this point described in one of the admirable poems of the great Jesuit poet, Gerard Manley Hopkins, as he reflects on the reality of the divine harvest, of nature, and of ourselves.

He reflects that all has been made ready by the many forces of nature and personal history. All creation stretches its capabilities to entice this sacred moment of grace into existence. Here are his wonderful words describing the moment before birth, before the harvest: "These things, these things were here and but the beholder/ Wanting; which two when they once meet/ The heart rears wings bolder and bolder/ And hurls for him, O half hurls earth for him off under his feet."[7]

The beholder wanting, needed, absolutely necessary for "it" to happen. To behold is to be held by the moment with all its content. It is also to be fully present, alert, and observant. That is a central part of marriage, the act of full responsibility: the mutual gift of self, given and received, from one to the other. It can happen in bed in their sexual embrace after a day of hard work. It can also happen as their eyes meet in love after the last child has gone to bed. It can happen across the breakfast table while sipping the wake-up flavor of freshly brewed coffee. The sacred encounter of marital life is "an anytime possibility." But to experience it, it's crucial to expect it, to anticipate its arrival, to desire it no matter what the cost, and to prepare one's mind and heart for it, and be ready to become beholders of each other's deep sacredness. To know each other is to experience such moments of mutual revelation and to accept with

---

[7] Gerard Manley Hopkins, "Hurrahing the Harvest," *Gerard Manley Hopkins: The Oxford Authors* (New York: Oxford University Press, 1986) 134.

an open mind and heart all that is revealed. Notice how the language of marital intimacy easily echoes religious language. The experience of God is quite available within the parameters of marriage, especially when we are seeking God in that setting. The fire of God's loving presence burns between husband and wife.

God rides upon love

Sacred times of deep encounter between persons are fleeting. They come and go, like so many of life's major moments. But they leave an impression. They transform our being. They can issue forth in events of personal conversion where the basic orientation of our life replaces some of our self-centeredness with an orientation devoted to another.[8] We become a more loving person. We have already discussed the love aspect of marriage in an earlier chapter, but here it's important to connect it specifically with marital spirituality. The heart of Christian spirituality is the experience of loving. That's true for all persons. And when part of marriage, it should have rigorous staying power, a shelf life that coincides with one's whole lifetime. It's rooted in a promise before God to have and to hold until death. Again, no small challenge.

Love is what holds people together, but especially in marriage. It's also the lifeline between us and God. All of this loving stuff carries connecting energy. As was said in the Gospels and in the early centuries of the church's life, God so loved the world that God elevated humanity to the level of our sharing in the divine. Especially through the life, death, and resurrection of Jesus, divine life, often referred to as sanctifying grace, flows into us making us adopted children of God. In the church we are now the terrestrial Body of Christ, and God's creation continues to unfold and develop through our good and loving thoughts, words, and deeds. The love life of God extends from God into the core of our being. The primary arena in which this happens is through the love between us humans. This was the primary message of the discourse at the Last Supper as reported in St. John's Gospel. Love one another as I have loved you. They will know you are mine by the love they witness between you, my disciples.

[8] This aspect of marriage is aptly described in Richard Gaillardetz, *A Daring Promise: A Spirituality of Christian Marriage* (New York: The Crossroads Publishing Company, 2002) 61–85.

What's important in marital spirituality is to dwell on the reality of marital love in all these magnificent dimensions. For instance, we do well to affirm that marital love is both fully human and authentically divine. We can reflect on the fact that we are like sacred vessels bearing God's life to each other. Simple as these affirmations are, they connect us with realities whose depth we can hardly imagine, though through faith we know them to be there. They are mysteries, meaning that their full truth can only be partially grasped by our finite minds. But in this case, even a little knowledge is of immense value.

God's love took on distinct human form in the person and life of Jesus. Early on, there was debate within the church as to whether Jesus was in fact fully human. Some said he was God, but only appeared as human. What was at stake in this debate was not just something about Jesus, but also about us. Did he have our thoughts, feelings, and re-actions? Did Jesus, in fact, truly become part of who we are? If he did, which we believe, then God decisively transformed human life, first in Christ Jesus and then in us. Humankind became not just a sophisticated form of the dust of the earth, but something essentially godly. This altera-tion of our humanity implies that while our created human life is part of the earth, it's more than that!

This has a decided effect on marriage. For no one will argue that ordinary marriage is not human. It's totally so! It has an unalterable human cast. This is exactly as God wanted it. While we are created by God as spiritual beings, we also are of flesh and blood. To be human is to be, at one and the same time, spiritual and corporeal. We can be said to be spiritual bodies and corporeal spirits. And we have to affirm all this and not try to turn ourselves into angels or to relate to each other as if we were not essentially bodily. I fully agree with those who decry any approach to the spiritual or Christian life that falls into the ancient heresy of dualism, which implies an essential separation or division within us, between body and soul.

I have been helped to understand a little of this quite complex reality by thinking about an analogical situation that has developed over the last few years in the medical world. Most will be familiar with what we call our psychosomatic condition where we affirm a pervasive connec-tion between our minds and bodies, a linkage that has now received a great deal of attention in the medical community.

My personal acquaintance with this connection of body and mind was heightened in recent years when I was diagnosed twice with severe arterial blockage in my heart that required the corrective procedure of angioplasty. Plaque buildup in the arterial walls can be caused by many things—unhealthy diet, including excessively fatty foods, a lack of physical exercise, genetic influences from parents, and extreme stress. After a lengthy interview with my cardiologist, we concluded that stress was the number one cause of my heart problems. My initial reaction to this diagnosis contained a bit of skepticism because I had difficulty imagining how something as immaterial as stress could cause such a material effect, plaque buildup in my heart. I was then given a short course on how the various systems of the human body interrelate, as understood by today's medical science. It turns out that our bodies are interlaced and connected by a very complex wiring system that creates a rather sophisticated connection between our mental and physical life. No reputable health care professional doubts this linkage. Nor do I.

So how does this help us understand spiritual life, including our relationship to God? Are there similar profound connections, however secretive they may be? The answer is fully in the affirmative. Of course, when calling to mind this deeper body and spirit connection, we enter the world of God's Spirit, as well as a dimension of ourselves that is fully dependent on God for every breath we take.

This spiritual world is incredibly pervasive and of singular importance when we think about the meaning and value of our lives both to ourselves, to those around us, and to God. We are beholding reality with a perspective of what the great Jesuit spiritual writer, Teilhard de Chardin, named the *divine* milieu. There we encounter the God who created all of us and are infused with God's love. This touches our humanity as we dwell in this very material world. The spiritual is welded by God to the material. The uncreated source supports the created. And our connection with God grows as we deepen our love for each other.

Let's focus on marriage now, knowing that within marriage, within all its utterly human and seemingly quite ordinary acts, there is God. And through marital love, even the smallest snippet of marital love, we connect with God. We sing, *ubi caritas et amor, deus ibi est* (where there is charity and love, there is God). In that spirit, Pope Benedict XVI began his first encyclical letter with the words of St. John's first letter, "God is love, and he who abides in love abides in God, and God in him" (1 John 4:16).[9]

---

[9] The whole letter is a profound meditation on love as the center of the Christian life. See his *Deus Caritas Est* (God is Love), December 25, 2005.

While his teaching is directed to all the members of the Catholic Church, the Pope briefly notes a special role for married love. "Marriage based on exclusive and definitive love becomes an icon of the relationship of God as his people and vice versa."[10] In the next chapter when we describe the sacramental dimension of Christian marriage, we will explore this divine-human connection between God and marriage more fully.

Let's return to the survey I mentioned at the beginning of this chapter. Sadly, no married person mentioned that in their experience of marital love, they experienced the presence of God. I cannot assign a failing grade to their response because I know from my own experience that such a sense of God's loving presence is neither clear nor obvious. It's a hidden presence. My own view would be that it takes a well-disciplined capacity for knowing to see that presence. We know that some of the saints of the church were able to penetrate the wrapping that conceals God within creation. But I would have to add that we can all work on this skill of discernment, this ability to see deeper.

Earlier we described the need for stillness and concentration to acquire some sense of God's presence in ourselves and others. Here I suggest using this process to focus on what freely is given and received in the marital love between wives and husbands. These acts, however small they may seem, contribute much to the substance of married life and its proper spirituality. Sometimes our awareness of love's presence comes more after we've had time to think about it. Our love creates memories. And revisiting these memories can release love's power in us even more.

Each marriage will have its own accounting of these expressions of love. We conclude this chapter by highlighting some typical gestures of love in marriage. They place us in a sacred space that exists between wife and husband. With each act of love, God becomes more and more a part of their shared life.

Actions graced and given

We now fill the rest of the canvas of marital spirituality with a little detail. That's often the last part of a painting. In portrait work, for ex-

---

[10] Pope Benedict XVI, *Deus Caritas Est*, section 11.

ample, the artist will add the distinctive lines of aging next to the eyes. Or the subtle complexities of complexion will be feathered into cheek and forehead. Sometimes variations in hair color will be carefully nuanced so as to repeat on canvas what's actually there in the person being portrayed. As is rightly said, it's all in the detail. We also complete the "know, love, serve" template referred to earlier by describing acts of loving service between the spouses.

In my earlier book on Christian marriage, I placed mutual acceptance as an important first step in spiritual advancement. Acceptance in marriage points to the often difficult, yet necessary, need for loving acceptance of each other for better or worse. It creates the rock solid foundation upon which marriage lasts. Marital acceptance includes a whole variety of ways we say to each other: I accept you as you are, your ideas and opinions, your quaint and sometimes annoying habits, your faults and even failures at times, in other words, all that is essentially *you*!

Note carefully that I didn't include *liking* all those personal qualities listed, but accepting them. It's also partly related to the difference between accepting someone as he or she is, versus reserving acceptance until that person changes into some image or likeness we might prefer. We've all heard or thought that our love is so strong that we want to make the other person better. Underneath that project lurks the reality of conditional acceptance, and that's exactly what weakens and can even destroy a marriage. It prevents love from being fully real.

Full acceptance of each other in marriage is quite challenging, especially given the inevitable differences between the spouses. And not all dissimilarities are known or even suspected at the time of the wedding. But as sure as the sun rises and sets each day, eventually the full spectrum of differences and even disagreements will come to the surface. I wonder whether the high rate of marital dissolution early on in a marriage is due to a severe lack of real acceptance.

Acceptance is the grounding force of the marriage. It dismisses the purely imaginative qualities of one's spouse and looks at the other with eyes fully open. Further, when the acceptance is genuine, it clearly places each spouse in a somewhat risky position. Who knows what tomorrow will bring? But that's the overwhelming power of acceptance in marriage. It's a bit like the poem of Robert Frost where he says that you know you're home when they have to take you in. While that image of acceptance may appear to carry mostly a sense of tolerance, the notion of assumed acceptance is important. Here, we're also describing thoughts, feelings, and actions that are positive and progressive. Acceptance willingly sees the past, present, and future and stretches forth its welcome and support. In marriage, many important relational benefits come from this kind of acceptance.

For instance, we all live with a bit of fear that if anyone really knew us in full, they might not like us. We put on our best when we appear in public. We carefully measure our words so as not to disturb others. But in marriage, more than anywhere else, we should feel that wondrous freedom to be ourselves, knowing that even on our worst day, we will still be welcomed and affirmed in love.

An essential feature of genuine love is the kind of love the New Testament refers to as *agape*. This is genuine altruistic love, a love for the other as other. Certainly a great test for our altruism is the wholehearted acceptance of our husband or wife in their totality. Again, this could almost be called a frightful challenge. In a sense, we exit the safe confines of our own world and enter into that of another. And in marriage, we take up residency there, as the wedding vows say, "until death do you part." We don't just visit like a tourist. We become a fulltime resident. Before long, we may find ourselves asking, who moved my toothbrush? Or even more telling, who changed my whole life?

Gestures of acceptance are many. Acknowledgment and compliments freely given about the other's appearance, accomplishments, ideas, and whatever it is that flows from the other's uniqueness all fill the bill. They bespeak the intrinsic value and beauty of the other person. It's important that they be genuine and real. Each act of acceptance clearly strengthens the marital bond. The conclusions drawn from the marital researcher, John Gottman, and others about successful marriages all corroborate the importance of deep and abiding acceptance.

Before moving to another aspect of acts or gestures inherent in marital spirituality, I want to add a word about perfection or idealism. Recall that we are discussing human gestures of marital spirituality. To be human is to be partial, imperfect, in process, and even to err at times. I'm not trying to offer an argument for imperfection or inadequacy, but simply to note that one of the essential aspects of being human is to be "on the way" or as it's said in spiritual discourse today, "on pilgrimage."

Occasionally, the church, along with experts in marital life, slip into idealistic language in spoken or written words. Too often, the rhetoric that calls us to be and to do better sounds like it invites us to the impossible. Like the following: Pray always! But how can I do this with a crying baby in the backseat during rush hour. Love your enemy! That's impossible for me right now. Someone offered drugs to my teenager yesterday. I want to wring his neck. Love your spouse, no matter what! Who can do that? He forgot my birthday yesterday. Not even a card! Life is filled with difficulties and even great saints had their bad days. All that God or anyone should ask is that we try. Sometimes we will register a success. Sometimes we won't. God always understands and God accepts us just the same.

Returning to our discussion of marital spirituality, it will also include the simple acts of helping each other in our day-to-day effort to survive. In the field of education, we hear of programs that aim to return to the basics. Good old reading, writing, and arithmetic. If you don't cover the basics, all the rest will be built on sand. Something similar can be said about marriage spirituality. It covers the basics.

Marital spirituality would include acts like sharing in child care, housework, earning a living, and whatever it takes us to make it through the day. And to follow the advice of many marriage therapists, this is not a fifty-fifty proposition. Rather it's a 100 percent calculation with both wife and husband fully involved in the daily challenges of living together. In fact, one sign of a good marriage is that the act of calculation hardly ever happens. It's beyond a counting game. Roles are flexible. The work can be arduous and messy. Shared effort is the best. What's important to appreciate here is that it's all part of marital spirituality.

The gospel is filled with invitations to feed the hungry, forgive those who have hurt us, share all that one has with the needy, reach out to all those who lack life's basic essentials. How might all this translate into marital life? What does hunger look like in a marriage? What about the need that arises when one's spouse is lonely, depressed, discouraged, or afraid? How often is forgiveness needed to heal a hurt, whether it was intended or not? What sensitive and loving married couples do is use their imagination to connect their faith with daily marital life.

We have hardly touched on the increased demands that come with having children. Thankfully we have mostly departed from the era when it was said that there was a boy for me and a girl for you. In marriage today, parenting is a shared vocation. All can be winners in this arrangement. But like the challenges of maintaining a vital marriage, being a parent these days is most demanding. Life has become much more complex as the requirements of jobs and homelife blend with countless other activities. This puts a strain on marriage, but once again, how these demands are handled contributes to the quality of the spiritual life of the married.

Marriage is ideally suited for creating outstanding saints. Following Christ and carrying our own crosses can happen every day in marriage. If history informs, we can conclude that few married couples will ever be found enrolled on the sacred registry of canonized saints in the church. I believe, however, that one of the surprises awaiting us in the next life is clear knowledge of what was really important and holy in this life. Getting up in the middle of the night to help a restless child or a wide-awake spouse may be among the most heroic sacred actions ever done!

In conclusion, part of any discussion of spirituality should include mentioning something about what is quite essential to the pursuit of deep holiness or spirituality, the act of prayer. I find it difficult and even dangerous to make sweeping generalizations about methods or styles of prayer for the married.

Prayer provides a much needed and a privileged access to the source of all our spiritual lives, God's Spirit dwelling with us. Yet the prayer life of the married will vary from couple to couple, from husband to wife. It must be authentic and not forced. It will arise from personal choice, the nature of their relationship along with their personal histories. Many couples live in what's called a marriage of mixed faith. This means that their faith is rooted in different religious denominations, and maybe cultural traditions. But I would like to suggest that we are all connected to the same God, however different might be the names we use or the traditions we practice. Mutual respect is essential in marriage and its role in formal or informal religious activities is important.

So I offer a simple suggestion. Pray together when you can. Pray for each other and your marriage every day. Be open to learn about God and what's connected to God from each other. Be accepting of both similarities and differences. Celebrate and support each other's relationship with God. God has created marriage as a fundamental way of uniting his beloved creatures in the service of enriching each other's lives and the lives they create and touch. That was number one on God's agenda. May we find it in our own marriages.

Chapter Eight

What makes marriage a sacrament?

When I first learned about the sacraments of the church, I was but a youngster in a Catholic school. We were given this little book that was called "the drill book." Basically it was filled with Catholic facts, especially those having to do with numbers. I recall the seven capital sins, three persons in God, nine first Fridays, two natures in Christ, ten commandments, six special precepts that were created by the church, fourteen stations of the cross, fifteen mysteries of the rosary, and so forth. Then there were the seven sacraments which were described as outward signs, instituted by Christ, to give grace. The nuns who taught us even held contests to determine who knew their facts the best, sort of an early version of Trivial Pursuit. I more or less assumed back then that all these collectives came from Christ himself, or perhaps Moses. It gave a certain amount of comfort knowing that we Catholics had all these "things from God" to help us get to heaven. Somewhere along the way I also learned that Protestants didn't have as many things. So Catholicism maintained a kind of lead in the church race because we had more sacred stuff.

Today, when I ask people why they remain Catholic even knowing of widespread clergy sexual abuse, they will often say that there's still the sacramental life of the church, and that's important to them. They are to me as well. Sacraments were and remain part of the church's bedrock because they connect us as humans to the person and work of God's Spirit. God connects with us and we connect with God in and through the sacraments.

When I studied theology in the seminary, and later as a doctoral student at Notre Dame, I learned that behind these "Catholic facts" were a mass of wonderful truths, along with some interesting and complex history. I found out that Jesus did not deliver a "drill book" to his disciples. But he did offer a perspective on God and creation that formed the basis of wonderful and challenging insights about the sacramental nature of God's world. Here we will be reflecting on the sacramental nature of Christian marriage. And we will learn that the search for ever deeper insight into its meaning is very much an ongoing process.

Every great idea, just like every person, has a history. The same can be said about how marriage came to be named one of the seven sacraments of the church. Some might be surprised to learn that it took the Catholic Church close to a millennium and a half to give marriage what, I would say, was its due. In affirming the sacramental aspect of Christian marriage, the church was officially saying that marriage among Christians was sacred, that it was intended by God to be not only a way to achieve closeness with God, but that it was a public symbol of something very profound, namely God's relationship with God's beloved, the members of the church. Sacraments are created human symbolic actions that make available and point to God's presence and power. And they have been created for us.

Gradually, the church took interest in creating a meaningful sacred rite to initiate marriage. That it took so long to bring marriage into the middle of church life suggests to me that the holiness of marriage may not be that obvious. Recall my earlier comments from the retreat I gave to married couples and how the attendees failed to readily see God's presence within their marital relationship.

When we examine the history of marriage as a sacrament, we learn that the church found at least some evidence that Jesus instituted the other six sacraments of the church. A few theologians believed that Jesus might have instituted matrimony at the marriage feast at Cana. That proved to be too much a stretch of the ecclesial imagination. The wedding feast at Cana is important not because Jesus "made" a sacrament there, but because it was the first great sign in St. John's Gospel that the kingdom of God was beginning. And Jesus was there to insure that there was enough wine to celebrate this. Marriage as part of God's world had a different kind of history. Unlike the other sacraments, marriage preceded the coming of Christ, going all the way back to the dawn of human time. I believe the names given to that first married couple were Adam and Eve.

The history of theological reflection on marriage in the church shows a great deal of uncertainty and debate.[1] At its low point, in the middle of the first millennium, marriage was only tolerated as something needed

---

[1] For a summary of this, see Peter Jeffery, *The Mystery of Christian Marriage* (New York/Mahwah: Paulist Press, 2006) 194–226.

for the continuation of family and humanity. It was not valued as a way to follow the full challenges of Jesus. Sacred virginity filled that role. There were times when the church taught that the only justification for sexual relations in marriage was to have children. Mostly, however, the church had very little to say about marriage.

There were a whole host of other reasons why the church was slow to sing its praises. In the period right after Christ's resurrection, there were serious expectations that he would soon return and that this world would end. Some saw marriage as an unnecessary complication, a sort of waste of time. Why not just stay single and wait prayerfully for the grand finale when Jesus would return fully victorious over evil? St. Paul seemed to share this view. Later, as the church used some of the indigenous philosophies of the day to explain its teachings, it began to divide creation into two parts. Anything related to the body (matter) was considered bad, and anything of the soul (spirit) was deemed good. Such an approach came largely from the philosophy of Platonism, which was quite popular among intellectuals of the third and fourth century.

The ideal of virginity also grew in importance. One theologian, the famous St. Jerome (340–420), who translated the Bible into Latin, held that one of the best things about marriage was that it produced more virgins for the church. A rather limited view of things, I would say. If marriage came into the church's conversation at all during these first few centuries, it was mostly to use it as an allegory of God's relationship to us. In itself, it was not considered that important.

St. Augustine of Hippo (354–440) accepted some of this anti-matter view early in his life, but later, after his conversion to Christianity, wrote about the goods of marriage. He listed it as "sacrament" but not in the sense of the formal rituals of the church. He saw it as a symbol of God's relation to us. That was an important addition to the theology of the church. He referred to the passage in the Epistle to the Ephesians where we read the following in referring back to what was said about Adam and Eve in Genesis. "For this reason [getting married] a man will leave his father and mother and be joined to his wife, and the two will become one flesh. This is a great mystery [this word in Greek is *mysterion* which will be translated into Latin as *sacramentum*], and I am applying it to Christ and the church."[2] This became the most important text we have for eventually establishing Christian marriage as sacramental. St. Augustine was at the threshold of seeing marriage as a sacrament, but he held back

[2] Eph 5:31-32.

because he still largely associated sexuality with sinfulness. His views on marriage prevailed for the next thousand years.

In brief, we can summarize the first fifteen hundred years of Christianity as affirming that marriage was good, but not the best way for Christians to live. Monasticism grew as the preferred way of life among Christians. Eventually, priests in the Roman Catholic Church were not allowed to marry. In the late middle ages, as the legal structures of the old Roman Empire began to crumble, the church took on a more active role of overseeing not just marriage, but many of the societal connections relating to its rights and responsibilities.

From a general view of history, many marriages within the church's realm were arranged, especially if title or land were involved. So-called common-law marriages were often the way of the peasant class. By the thirteenth century, theologians were beginning to list Christian marriage or matrimony as one of the sacraments of the church. But it was not until the sixteenth century at the Council of Trent that the Roman Catholic Church, largely in response to the view of some reformers who claimed that there were only two sacraments, Baptism and the Eucharist, formally declared that there were seven sacraments, and that Matrimony was one of them. It also legislated that marriage should take place in the church before a priest and two witnesses. Clandestine marriages at that time were a pastoral concern.

From then on the church looked upon marriage mostly from a legalistic point of view. The church defined the nature of marriage, determined who could marry and who could not, and it described the required dispositions necessary to enter marriage. Up until recent times, most church experts in Christian marriage wore the hats of canon lawyers. This need not to be thought of in negative terms, but it shows that the church's official thinking about marriage was mostly from a legalistic and liturgical perspective. That began to change in the twentieth century when views from trained theologians, who were also married, began to write about Christian marriage using a broader spiritual and theological perspective. One might add, they also possessed the experiential insights to deepen their understanding of this sacrament.[3]

Like many other aspects of contemporary church life, a significant breakthrough concerning marriage was expressed in the documents of Vatican II, especially in the section on Christian marriage and family life in *The Pastoral Constitution on the Church in the Modern World*. There we read,

[3] See Dietrich von Hildebrand, *Marriage* (New York: Longmans, 1942) and Herbert Doms, *The Meaning of Marriage* (New York: Sheed and Ward, 1939).

"Spouses, therefore, are fortified and, as it were, consecrated for the duties and dignity of their state by a special sacrament; fulfilling their conjugal and family role by virtue of this sacrament, spouses are penetrated with the Spirit of Christ and their whole life is suffused by faith, hope and charity; thus they increasingly further their own perfection and their mutual sanctification, and together they render glory to God."[4]

One can almost feel fresh air flowing around these words, perhaps a little of that air Pope John XXIII hoped for when he figuratively opened the windows of the church at the beginning of the council. To continue this positive approach, instead of couching the reality of Christian marriage in terms of dangers and difficulties, it was given a positive framework. It was as if the wind was blowing from behind, moving marriage into its rightful place as a very important expression of the Christian life of holiness and sanctity. I especially appreciate the notion of "mutual sanctification" in this Vatican II passage, an idea we touched on in the last chapter. It deserves our full attention.

To develop an understanding of the sacramental nature of Christian marriage for today, I want to examine it from two perspectives. First I will connect marriage with patterns in creation itself, dimensions of which go back literally to the beginning. Within the church, this approach toward understanding has been respected as a fruitful way of knowing God. It's been referred to as looking at God in the book of nature (creation). Knowledge gained in that context can then be connected with the knowledge of God as revealed in the Bible, especially through the life, words, and work of Jesus. What can be done, I believe, is to show that the understanding of marriage we gain from creation can strengthen and deepen what we learn from its specifically Christian context. Catholicism holds that grace builds on nature and that we can effectively use the natural world as a stepping-stone to God.

That's at the heart of the sacraments of the church. Water for baptism. Bread and wine for the Eucharist. Oil for the sacrament of the sick. And for Christian marriage? The couple themselves, joined in the service of love and life. Another way of saying this is that marriage as intended in God's creation already had a kind of sacramental identity from the beginning. Not just the beginning of human history, but even before that. Well before! My approach in this matter will be more existential than legal, more experiential than abstract. We'll be using a method of analogy, which implies a movement from what's seen to what's unseen, what's

---

[4] Vatican II, *Gaudium et Spes* (The Pastoral Constitution on the Church in the Modern World), section 48.

in creation to what's connected with God. This way of discovery has been used in the church for centuries.

Marriage and sacramental creation

If we look at creation, like St. Augustine did, looking for signs of God, we can find them everywhere. All creation ultimately came from the mind and heart of God. Or as we say in the Nicene Creed, all things seen and unseen. So with the right frame of mind, and with God's grace that is always there, we could potentially "see" God in anything and everything that was good.

I'm not saying that we can directly see God, or peer into God's mind, but the more we understand the nature of the created cosmos, the closer we seem to get to where Albert Einstein hoped to find God's very thoughts, especially what God thought at the very beginning of creation. Recall what's written in Genesis, when God looked over all that was created, especially humankind, and God immediately proclaimed that it was "very good." Something very important was "there." Something about God. Something we should investigate not just out of curiosity, not just to use for our purposes, but to gain insight into the "big picture," which is how God sees it.

Today, we look at this same creation with some new eyes, especially through the wondrous inventions of high-powered microscopes and telescopes. Incredible and enticing mysteries of nature unfold before us every day. I have had an interest in cosmology, the study of the nature of the universe, and especially its history for many years. While I am not a professional scientist, I can appreciate some of what's reported. I enjoy the role of being an informed amateur, a word that carries the notion of being someone who loves what's learned. For example, I am deeply touched by what's now coming to light using astronomical instruments and sophisticated computers that describe what has been happening at each period during the amazing history of our universe. We can now describe in rich detail much of what has happened all the way to within less than a second from the moment of the initial big bang. The closer we get to understanding the absolute beginning, the more we gain insight into what we experience today. We grasp a little of its long history.[5]

---

[5] For a compelling comprehensive description of this history, see Brian Swimme and Thomas Berry, *The Universe Story: From the Primordial Flaring Forth to the Ecozoic Era—a Celebration of the Unfolding of the Cosmos* (New York: HarperSanFrancisco, 1992).

Allow me to share some simple scientific findings about the early history of the universe that, I believe, shed a bit of light on the nature of marriage—which, of course, came *much* later. Today we know which element constitutes most of the known matter in the cosmos, unless you include dark matter of which we know very little. It's the element hydrogen, each atom of which is composed of one proton and one electron. When I studied chemistry and physics many years ago, we were taught that hydrogen was as basic as one could get. In that understanding, God would be thought of as having created hydrogen atoms first. Nowadays, that's as true as are all those theories of a flat earth!

All atoms, we now know, are composed of almost countless sub-atomic particles. Some call them "strings" containing both mass and energy, but describing that level of created reality would take us away from our topic. So let's return to hydrogen.

To my surprise, I learned recently that our universe was almost a billion years old before the first hydrogen atom came into being. Before then, the universe was too hot and there was too much movement for its various component parts to connect. A potential hydrogen nucleus with its proton could not even connect with an electron to form a molecule of hydrogen. There was no "place" to meet. To use a crude, but I think helpful image, it would be like going to a very busy, lively, and noisy rock concert and trying to meet someone new. If you cannot even hear yourself think because of the uproar, there's no possibility that you could carry on a decent conversation. So no meaningful connection is possible.

But finally, conditions were favorable. The grand meeting of proton and electron happened and because of what's called the evenness of the expanding universe, it happened all over the place almost simultaneously. Differences at this very basic level between the proton and electron were overcome, and union took place. The two became one. Then, give or take a few million years, a second meeting took place, this time between two hydrogen atoms forming the hydrogen molecule. Again, two became one. And finally, the most powerful event of all came about, the coming together and uniting of two hydrogen molecules with the result that burning bright stars came into being! The lights were turned on in the up-to-then absolutely dark universe. Nuclear fusion happened. Two became one. A new helium molecule was created by their union and in the process bright energy was released. Energy that was needed for all the rest to come about, including us! And because of nuclear fusion, the galaxies, the stars, their planets

and moons, and everything else came forth in a form about the way
they look today.[6]

Around four billion years ago our current solar system was born.
Our Brother Sun flared forth. The earth congealed and grew from the
gravitational attraction between countless particles of stardust that were
left over from an earlier stellar explosion. The earth's temperature was
brought to just the right level so that hydrogen could combine with a
host of other elements like oxygen and carbon, and eventually create
living beings. Then, one bright spring day (that's just a guess), an Adam
met an Eve and they said to each other, "Let's get married." All creation
immediately cheered.

Well, you can write that story however you wish, but I would insist
that the basic process include the uniting of individual parts in forming
something much greater, more complex, and more wondrous than existed
before. That's the pattern embedded in God's creation.

The research and discoveries that have given to us this fairly complete history of our universe is, I believe, the greatest scientific advance
of our time. And as I'm telling it here, which admittedly is only a small
part of the whole story, I only want to note that the joining of "two into
one" is a process that truly goes to "the heart of the matter." It changes
those who unite, perfects them in ways well beyond their individual
capacities, and transforms the whole of creation.

Further, this bit of science underscores how everything is related to
everything else. Einstein, along with thousands of scientists after him,
is right. There are no isolated atoms, nor are there isolated persons. We
are created by God in the deepest part of our being as social. And one
of the places where our social existence is most pronounced and inten-
sively experienced is in the relationship of marriage. It's also important
to add that it's through the love and the union achieved between the
wife and husband that new human life is created and develops. That's
nature's way. While there's massive debate these days about various
aspects of the procreation of new life, the fundamental, and I would add,
the preferred way this should occur is within a loving marriage.

All of what I've shared in this section of our investigation can be
read in the book of nature. But God also became human to offer us further
clarity about the intent and plan of God in creating us. Through God
being with us in Christ Jesus, through all that he said and did, our salva-

---

[6] To learn more about this, see Adam Frank, "The First Billion Years," *Astronomy*,
34:6, June, 2006, 30–35.

tion and sanctification became possible. God's light enlightened our darkness. In the final section of our discussion about the challenge of Christian marriage, we will say something about how the message of Jesus sheds even more light on the sacramental aspect of Christian marriage.

Marriage as Christian

St. John's Gospel begins with the astounding declaration that God's Word became flesh. In a sense, all the other "words" ever communicated by God to humankind were focused like a laser beam on and through the person of Jesus. In Jesus, the way to all the truth about life was there. God's revelation became personal. The proper faith response to God became personal. And through the person of Jesus, the firstborn of the New Creation, all creation, including marriage, was transformed. In a sense, all authentic religion became fully personal and interpersonal. But more about that in a minute.

Jesus once told a fascinating story to illustrate something about life in God's kingdom. He said that there was a very important wedding feast planned. The list of guests was carefully put together because it was the wedding of the king's son. But when the door opened for the guests to enter, no one was there. Not a single soul. The king then sent out a second invitation (perhaps the first one was mislaid), but those invited all had excuses for not coming. This really bothered the king so he sent out soldiers to kill those first invited. I don't know exactly what that meant except that it showed really deep disappointment on the part of the king. Eventually the king decided to forget about protocol, forget about the social registry, and open the doors to everyone. "Go therefore into the main streets, and invite everyone you find to the wedding banquet. Those slaves went out into the streets and gathered all whom they found, both good and bad; so the wedding hall was filled with guests."[7]

Like all of the stories or parables of Jesus, we can find rich food for thought in them. Often we need to read them a few times, think about them, even pray about them. Vatican II said that God's Spirit addresses us through the biblical word, so we pay extra close attention. We get a glimpse of what Jesus came to share with us in the parable of the wedding feast for the king's son.

[7] Matt 22:9-10.

So let's examine this parable a little further. Wedding feasts in biblical times were huge social events. Scholars tell us that they could last for days! We're talking about a celebration with a capital "C"! And if it was the wedding of the son of a king, well, this was an event no one would want to miss. Thus, the irony. Everyone on the A list of guests decided that staying with the banalities of their ordinary life, the humdrum of the office, weeding the fields, washing clothes, maybe even watching TV (if it had been available back then) was more important than attending the party of the century! The Gospel of Matthew is very good on dramatics.

We then learn that a revised list of invitees was prepared, which was not really a list but an open invitation to anyone who wanted to come. We are told that the servants of the king went out to the streets and indiscriminately invited everyone they encountered. Can you imagine what that kind of a net would drag in? If the new guests were just hanging around on the street corners, they could be anyone! But that's the point. Everyone was welcome. The king was a very generous person and a bit of a risk taker.

There was one catch, though. You had to come on your own. The invitation demanded a response. Later in the story we find out that you had to attend wearing a wedding garment. Important events required a little extra decorum. We're told that one fellow failed to cooperate with the dress code. In the end, he probably wished he had.

This story tells us something rather remarkable about God. We don't need a degree in advanced biblical studies to figure out that this parable about God's kingdom describes how God operates. God wants everyone to come to the feast. The feast is part of life in God's kingdom, and we know from other words of Jesus, it has already begun. There's a compelling feeling of inclusiveness and openness about the parable. The desire of the king is to reach out and include everyone, the good and the bad. That covers it all. And when a wedding feast is used as a kind of metaphor for life with God, it means good times for all.[8]

With the coming of Jesus, everything changes. That includes marriage. All interpersonal life becomes very important. Love between humans comes to be center stage. Final judgment of humankind revolves around how we respond to each other's needs. Love of God is perva-

---

[8] For a most interesting interpretation of this parable, see John Shea, *The Spiritual Wisdom of the Gospels for Christian Preachers and Teachers: On Earth as It is in Heaven, Year A* (Collegeville: Liturgical Press, 2004) 297–301.

sively connected with love of neighbor. Love between followers of Jesus becomes the great sign of authentic discipleship. The great sacramental events connect life with love. Just like a wedding feast.

It's not more than a short step from this valuing of interpersonal life to affirm the importance and the value of the marriage relationship. When God loves, life comes into being. All life! We are all here, as were all who came before us and after us, because God loved us first! God says the opening word in the creative conversation of life. But God employs humans to express additional words. The primary word of marriage is one of love, a total statement of love. That's where, for instance, the full expression of love involving human sexuality comes into play. As the church has taught through the centuries, marital love expressed in sexual union should be open to new life. Just as God's love is generative of life, so too is human love in marriage. That's why all of marriage is sacramental.

A couple's human manifestations of love, given through body and spirit, are also expressions of God's love. In Christian marriage, the couple gift each other in a deeply, sexually personal way and in a thousand other ways, too. Love is expressed in mutual care and assistance year after year. And while the wedding is the formal beginning of marriage, the loving acts that embody their mutual love continue. That means the whole of marital life can be sacramental. It can be a continuous manifestation of divine life wrapped in totally human form.

Having described this understanding of the sacramental side of marriage, I have to be honest and at least wonder whether all this wonderful meaning is widely known. I know it's there in church documents although these documents often sound more like legal briefs than love letters. Maybe the church should have gifted poets write its documents, especially those dealing with the complexities and depth of interpersonal life. Jesus had this gift of communication. He used stories, images, and symbols, and a variety of symbolic gestures to communicate the mystery of God that was at the depth of all that was. The church as a whole is constantly challenged to refine its language to more adequately capture what we as Christians experience and understand. Sometimes words are not enough, so we express ourselves through meaningful gestures. That's why surprise gifts, unexpected acts of kindness and affirmation, and endearing words can be so important in marriage. And in other relationships, too.

If we are attuned to God's presence in our ordinary lives (no small matter, to be sure), we will see the many gifts that come to us all the time.

God is always there, but as mentioned earlier, just a little under the surface. We need reminders. For some, a near death moment can awaken a new sense of life as God's gift. While I'm not trying to sell this practice, I find it helpful to keep what I call a surprise log, an accounting of God's gifts that seem to me, at least, as an extra bonus in life. It may be as ordinary as two sunny days in a row, which can be a real oddity during midwinter where I live in northwest Montana. Last evening, two large Canadian geese paraded their four new little ones across our backyard. Beholding that simple spectacle reminded me of our family and others we know and how we parade through life. The more we are alert to seeing God's gifts, the more we will notice.

The sacrament of Christian marriage contains the central mystery of faith: God loves us and creates us. The big bang, looked at in faith, becomes the Big Gift. God invites us in on the great human project through creating a social reality that unites woman with man for the whole of life. This involves a joining of persons for their own sake and for the sake of those that their life will touch.

A final thought about the personal aspect of this. Above we noted that when the Word became flesh in Jesus, all that was communicated by God through creation and through history, especially through that of Abraham and Sarah and their descendants, was suddenly concentrated within the person of Jesus. Jesus became God "on the move" through all the events reported in the Gospels, and through a few thousand other events that weren't recorded. To encounter Jesus was to have face-to-face contact with God in a totally human way. From Gospel reports, we know that some came to know this mystery and some didn't. And most likely, even those who had some inkling of the immense importance of meeting Jesus might also have been assailed by second thoughts or doubts. We see this wonderfully described in the story of doubting Thomas after the Resurrection of Jesus. He wanted more proof than just the word of his buddies.

To continue his presence in the world, Jesus created certain actions which, in a sense, kept him "there" on earth and active in the community. The most important of these activities is the celebration of the Eucharist, the breaking of the bread as it has sometimes been called. Remembering Jesus through doing what he did at the Last Supper was not just historical remembering as in "let's do what he did." No, done in faith and love, Jesus was there among them in the form of food for their journey ahead. Today the church speaks of the "real presence" of Jesus in the Eucharist. And Jesus is there in the other sacraments, too.

This personal presence of Christ Jesus through sacramental enactment is one of the more important theological developments of recent years. Vatican II taught that sacraments invite the whole community to participate and be active within the sacramental rituals. Every sacramental moment contains a kind of invitation to come and meet Jesus. Sometimes the church has to remind us of this because we forget. We also live in a culture which seems to have lost its sense of God in everyday life. Some would say this can even happen while we are engaged in activities that are expressly religious.

The church, to use a current image, seemed like a space station positioned halfway between heaven and earth. Sacramental experiences were like momentary trips from earth to heaven. Sacred moments were sharply separated from profane ones. There was little connection between sacraments and everyday experiences. This led to the sacraments of the church being not so much actions pointing to the Christian meaning of life on earth, but rather events that lifted us away from earth into a more sacred or divine space. When Christians entered wondrous churches they were led to believe that they were in some sense entering a space akin to heaven on earth.[9] I know that I'm describing a most complex matter but it's important to get this description on the table because this separation or distancing of what's human from what's Christian has had a direct effect of how marriage was thought of as a sacrament. We still see remnants of this view when people talk about Christian marriage as if its whole meaning and significance happened only at the time of the wedding.

Think of it this way. Jesus came to *this* earth to be available to humankind, to give his life for all of us. He wanted us to know about God and connect with God through earthly experiences. Heaven was planted on earth. This purpose was not lost with his Resurrection. In fact, he continued being present through the faithful, trusting, and loving actions of his disciples, then and now. Encountering Jesus remained possible, but now it happened especially in those actions of the church called sacraments.[10] In other words, the church and its activities, especially its sacramental ones, were not to pull us away from earth or from each other,

---

[9] For a richly detailed historical account of this separation of heaven from earth, see Bernard J. Cooke, *The Distancing of God: The Ambiguity of Symbol in History and Theology* (Minneapolis: Fortress Press, 1990).

[10] See the brilliant account of this aspect of sacramental life in E. Schillebeeckx, *Christ the Sacrament of the Encounter with God* (New York: Sheed and Ward, 1963).

but rather to ground us in the sacred, grace-empowered life that is ours right now and will continue to be even after we die.

The presence and power of God also entered Christian marriage. And while it took the church a long time to acknowledge this, eventually it did. Through the marital vows of promise given before God and the church, including one's family and friends, through the unique gift of self that is embodied in the expression of bodily, sexual love, through the many acts of love in word and deed that pass between the husband and wife throughout their shared life, through the ups and downs that seem an essential part of terrestrial life, through efforts to share what's within us and lighten each other's burdens, through it all, married couples enjoy sacramental existence, God with and in them, and most of all, actively loving them as they love each other. They experience the love of God in a privileged way, through their mutual love of each other.

God's gift of life includes a grand love story filled with surprises and one great challenge: To love each other as Christ Jesus has and continues to love us. And this can even happen (in fact, it does!) in Christian marriage.

Suggested Readings

Coontz, Stephanie, *Marriage, a History: From Obedience to Intimacy or How Love Conquered Marriage*, New York: Viking, 2005.

Gaillardetz, Richard, *A Daring Promise: A Spirituality of Christian Marriage*, New York: The Crossroad Publishing Company, 2002.

Gottman, John M. *The Seven Principles for Making Marriage Work*, New York: Crown Publishers Inc., 1999.

Heskin, Kathy, *Marriage: A Spiritual Journey*, Mystic: Twenty-Third Publications, 2002.

Jeffery, Peter, *The Mystery of Christian Marriage*, New York/Mahwah: Paulist Press, 2006.

Lawler, Michael, *Marriage and the Catholic Church: Disputed Questions*, Collegeville: Liturgical Press, 2002.

Post, Stephen G., *Unlimited Love: Altruism, Compassion and Service*, Philadelphia and London: Templeton Foundation Press, 2003.

Stanley, Scott, *The Heart of Commitment: Compelling Research Reveals the Secrets of a Lifelong, Intimate Marriage*, Nashville: Thomas Nelson Publishers, 1998.

Thatcher, Adrian, *Marriage after Modernity: Christian Marriage in Postmodern Times*, New York: New York University Press, 1999.

Wallerstein, Judith S., and Sandra Blakeslee, *The Good Marriage: How and Why Love Lasts*, Boston and New York: Houghton Mifflin Company, 1995.

Index